Raw, honest, erotic and beautiful. There are moments when the lyricism of the writing stops you in your tracks. To use Caroline Bobby's own words – it is a letter from the simplicity of her heart.

Author of Letters of a Dissatisfied Woman:
The Fine Art of Complaining

Caroline is possessed by an uncommon depth of observation and a use of the English language that might call into question the very way a reader sees their own life. Such observation appears to have come from a living of life right up to the very edge of death, and back. And on more than one occasion. Her life is a mysterious and unimaginable journey to a home few could imagine, and her writing a privileged front passenger seat to it all.

Nic Askew – Soul Biography's Inner View

*Scribbled life laid bare,
tenderness blooms through the scars,
beauty born of pain*

Anna Gekoski – BA, MPhil (Cantab.), MSc, PhD.
Murder by Numbers: British Serial Sex Killers Since 1950 (1998)
What's Normal Anyway? Celebrities' Own Stories of
Mental Illness (2014)
Victims and Survivors' Own Stories of Intrafamilial Child
Sexual Abuse (2020)
(with Steve Broome)

I've long known Caroline to be deeply compassionate, kind, and articulate. After reading Postcards from a Little Life, I can only echo Leonard Cohen's message to her:

> *"Deeply touched*
> *More than I can say here.*
> *Thank you."*

Allan Showalter MD – Webmaster of Cohencentric.com

Postcards from a Little Life is not an easy book to categorise. Sometimes memoir, sometimes poetry, but ultimately a fusion of both. It is raw, tender, and entirely its own. Caroline Bobby writes with poignant honesty about the 'ordinary' things of life, friendship, cats and dogs, alongside the themes others often edit out: addiction, sex work, pain, depression, and death Beneath it all, strong threads weave this beautiful book together. One is Caroline's deep vulnerability; her longing is boundless, another is her love of beauty and the power of the written word. She harnesses both, and Postcards from a Little Life is what she made.

I read it in one sitting, sometimes wiping away tears, sometimes laughing, sometimes noticing my jaw drop in surprise. Most of all, feeling reconnected with a love for life in all its paradoxes, and a sense of self-compassion.

Alex Svoboda, PhD – founder of freedomDANCE,
author of 'Action-Oriented Mindfulness'

Postcards from a Little Life

by
Caroline Bobby

Edited by
Rose Rouse

Art by
Asanga Anand

© Caroline Bobby, 2025

Published by Cracked Publishing

All rights reserved. No part of this book may be reproduced, adapted, stored in a retrieval system or transmitted by any means, electronic, mechanical, photocopying, or otherwise without the prior written permission of the author.

The rights of Caroline Bobby to be identified as the author of this work have been asserted in accordance with the Copyright, Designs and Patents Act 1988.

All the content from Déjà vu cards is used with permission from Advantages Of Age, where it was originally published.

The words from Kae Tempest's song People's Faces, on pages 38, 42 and 224, are used with permission from Kae Tempest.

Author photo © Andrew Hassenruck

A CIP catalogue record for this book is available from the British Library.

ISBN 978-1-0685025-0-7

Typeset by Clare Brayshaw

Manufacturer: York Publishing Services Ltd
64 Hallfield Road, Layerthorpe, York YO31 7ZQ
Tel: 01904 431213 | Email: enquiries@yps-publishing.co.uk
Website: www.yps-publishing.co.uk

Represented by: Authorised Rep Compliance Ltd.
Ground Floor, 71 Lower Baggot Street, Dublin D02 P593, Ireland
www.arccompliance.com

Dedicated to:

Tim Foskett
Sue Rickards
Joanna Watters

Thank you for being a tripod of scaffolding and support. While I could fill a few pages with gratitude and names, it is the scaffolding you have provided that has held and helped me build my home address – the one inside. I couldn't have done it without you.

Foreword

I think of Caroline as my sister – my writing sister. Our relationship exists not so much in the geographical world, in which we face towards each other from north-west to south-east across the great divide of The River, but in the heartlands of some inner and more mysterious place. In geo world we have seldom (but deeply) met and always, I think, on conscious dance floors. In the heartlands we live in two interconnected chambers, oxygenated by the same blood.

We are both reluctant writers, often hobbled and gagged. We stumble into words as a last resort, a little stunned, brought to our knees. A book is a shining miracle, a pilgrim diary of all the places where we broke and then looked up and saw the stars.

We write, in a way, from very different situations: Caroline from the landscape of a trauma survivor, a bed, a window ledge; I from the territory of autism and hypermobility, from my body in moving spaces; Caroline *half in love with easeful Death*; and I forever enamoured with the rumbling tumble of life. But there's a surprising amount of common ground, a shared sensibility, a series of echoes and reflections, as if we were refracted images of each other – another other.

I'm very happy that Caroline has created this book of moments, this little pile of unearthed shards that don't exactly make a pot but invite us to fill in the spaces. I think the requirement for this act of imagination is important because it asks us to bring something of our own, which yields into a sense of the commonality of our experiences, inevitably not quite the same, but also inevitably exactly so.

Postcards from a Little Life isn't dark, but it isn't light either. Caroline's great gift to us is her willingness to show us her woundedness, to show us the places where she barely made it through, to show us that there are many ways of thriving, and some of them are quiet and a little bit cracked and gaping, but still full of wonder, even if sometimes shot through with pain.

This is writing for healing clearly, but *Postcards from a Little Life* is so much more than a therapeutic journal. This is art. The writing is simple and exquisite. It ruffles us with gentle fingers. It wakes us up. This is also a meditation on the ongoing process of being alive, even if sometimes only marginally; on being in the moment, and not being in the moment, and remembering that it's possible to be in the moment. This is a very human book.

You could say, as Caroline does, that hers is a little life, but I don't think so. Caroline touches people in deep places, and she has touched many people. Be that through words or dancing or food, she is an artist of profound and meaningful connection. Those connections spread wide through the arteries of our communities. This beautiful, vulnerable book is another pulse of that life-giving blood. May it bless each life it touches. May it travel strong.

Jess Glenny is a movement teacher, facilitator, therapist, and author of *Ravelled Up: A Journey into Embodiment* (Embodied Press 2022).

My Little Life in Parts

Letter	1
Déjà vu cards	13
Small stories	49
Something like poems	83
Postcards to others – some sent – some not	141
Stroking naked men tales	161
Frontline	181
Acknowledgements	262

Letter

I nearly died on my thirtieth birthday.
Thirty years later, I nearly died again.

Both of these near deaths were defined by self-execution, although the passage of three decades between made everything different.

I had, without conscious thought or any kind of plan, forged a trajectory towards the sun; a city full of beaches, and as far away from everything I thought could be left behind in piles of old boxes stuffed with suffering, self-hatred, self-medication that was failing, and darkness that defied description.

I landed in the most beautiful city I could ever have dreamed. Sydney, Australia, around 1980. Somehow, I managed to shape my sorry self into the semblance of disguise. It was as intoxicating as hell. It was light. Pulsating with light. I fooled everyone except the part of me that knew as soon as the drugs that glued the part-I-was-playing started to dissipate, I wasn't real anymore. I kept that under fragile wraps and became a journalist for a little while in the burning white light of Sydney.

It was just before the AIDS epidemic arrived and drove a stake through the heart of Gay Pride, activism, hedonism, creative libidinal joy and dance floors that broke you wide open. I wrote a few things that mattered, all lost in the mists of time and distance. Too many funerals and too many drugs.

Decades of healing began the day I turned thirty.

Utterly lost on the streets of Sydney, a long fall from the grace of being a respected journalist and an activist in the Queer Community, I wasn't even a functional sex worker. The kinder of my regular sex-in-cars clientele just gave me money without the sex, while the less kind drove on by with disgust and horror in their eyes.

I had lost it.

I stumbled around the streets of Kings Cross and Darlinghurst in a full-blown psychotic break. I thought I was in a movie that everyone else had the script for. I could hear everybody else's thoughts, and was reading messages in street signs and car number plates. It is still strangely vivid, though I have no memory whatsoever of calling my ex-partner from four years earlier, and asking her to help me. She had drawn a line in the sand, having made many futile attempts to get me off drugs, and said, *Get clean or I'm done*. I never paused for a second to consider getting clean.

Much later, she told me that she'd come to my street-hooking-spot opposite Sydney Fire Station and I'd tried to get her into cars for a three-way. I don't remember ever seeing her. The anaesthesia of heroin. I don't remember so very many things, but I must have remembered she'd said to call her if I were ever ready to go to detox. I made a decision that night, down deep below the crazy, in a place I couldn't even hear yet, a choice to stay in this world. It turned out to be my thirtieth birthday.

It was hell for a long time.

The detox and rehab followed the 12-step recovery model, and sent us to Narcotics Anonymous meetings. It was my first experience of people coming together in a room to sit and share themselves. A kind of group. A kind of circle. All these years later, I can see and appreciate what a doorway that was. My first taste of a safe place.

This fluency of understanding and gratitude is retrospective. It was hell for a long time.

A year and a half into recovery, the fact I'd been in Australia for nearly seven years on a six-month visa caught up with me and I was evicted back to my homeland. It was a shock.

My mother had died while I was lost on the sunny side of the world. I am quite sure there's a direct link between her death and my not dying. Even though I didn't know, some animal part of me knew, and it was another doorway. On a more pragmatic note, she had left me some money and that was a blessing. It meant I could lurch about in what felt like very alien geography and try to find my feet.

London.
Bedsit.
Narcotics Anonymous every day.

I missed the light, the heat, the beaches, the Aussie voices, my recovery friends. All I knew to do was go to NA meetings, so I went to a lot. In many ways it was still hell, but I'd got the hang of a few things, and I hadn't had a drug or a drink for a year and a half. I grasped the one-day-at-a-time thing, and if I look back at myself from here, I appreciate my dogged spirit, my life force, whatever it was that kept me rolling forwards in the utterly foreign country of my own un-medicated pain.

As many have said before me, I couldn't have done it without the 12 Step Fellowship. It is an extraordinarily simple structure that holds, supports and welcomes all the crazy and wretched. There are no leaders, but the principles and guidelines create a safe harbour; the elders help the newcomers, and then they help the new newcomers. It is community. It is an invitation to show up and be lost, and in doing so discover that you are not alone. It was my first taste of home, of being seen and heard, and of connection with other humans without any drugs to make me brave or convince me I was okay.

People spoke about going to therapy.
I went too.
It was still hellish, but I now knew I wasn't alone. That, and only that, made staying here in this world, without a clue about how not to feel hellish, possible.

The distance, not three decades passing, but the distance from that initial cracking open – a very different kind of broken than the violence I had occupied from first breath.

My family of origin is one of those that looked very nice on top.
Middle class, though my mother never forgave my father for taking her down a few rungs of that ladder of status – from the edges and overlap of upper class, to something more ordinary, though still laden with privilege and advantage. It wasn't nearly so nice underneath.
I was the eldest, the first born. My brother came over three years later.

I'm going to offer you the haiku version of the life and times – aged 13 I sit in a very old school psychiatrist's office. My parents sit either side of me. It is a big, old-school, doctor desk. The caricature, old-school psychiatrist looks me up and down. He says: *Well, young lady, what seems to be the problem?*

I don't know how to answer, so I say what's true. The only true I know. I say something like: *It's all wrong at home.*

Psychiatrist looks at the parents flanking me, mostly it must be said at my father. He asks – is there a problem at home? My father says: *No. The problem is our daughter.*

I do know, as I remember the deepest dark of my first three decades. It was so dark I couldn't see anything at all. I have a language now for all sorts of why and how – I needed to find a map of some kind to translate and understand, at least enough to stumble through that cracking, to stay, knowing nothing. Feeling nothing except the beyond words agony of not taking drugs.

The thing that made it possible was that in those meetings I couldn't not see, or not know, that I was in good company. I literally took that first and life-changing medicine in rooms full other humans, all in their own way suffering and healing.

Now, in 2024, writing and feeling from here, I lose words for that distance, and the hate that nearly killed me. Narcotics Anonymous was where I fell through that initial cracking. I had made an inaudible choice, and there was somewhere to fall into a humanity I had literally never tasted. The dark was so dark because there was just no one else there.

I cannot tell you that I am, all these years later, free from the realms of darkness. I can tell you that I have discovered the darkest dark has threads of luminosity running through it, and that freedom is not what I imagined it to be at all.

I am an infinite vessel of gratitude.
I have had so much help, and I have needed every micro speck of it.

I often speak of homecoming, pilgrimage, crawling, stumbling, falling and finding a way to lumber on.

I was going to write books.
I didn't.

Many, many miles later, the impetus to make this book has something to do with being given a reprieve from the need to take my life. I tapped out these words as the first signs of spring 2021 were doing their beautiful thing. The world had been dealing with COVID-19 and in London, UK, we were emerging from lockdown. I was finding out what matters now that I had some more time to be here, alive, and breathing air in and out of my lungs.

I had a plan, and had it gone to plan, it would have resulted in my dying just about then. I made a choice that turned out to be deeply simple. If spinal surgery did not improve constant and acute pain that meant surviving and enduring the journey through each and every day, I would use that agency of choice and end it.

I decided to make an enquiry into the option of taking my life and make it public. I don't know much, but I do trust my sense that part-of-what-I'm-supposed-to-do-with-my-little life is talk and write about my specialist subjects – depression and death. I have a different take and a small contribution to offer to the discourse. So, I do that. I blog and write articles. I bring my voice to conversations that may not be expecting such a perspective.

With my dear friend (Andrew Hassenruck), maker of extraordinary films that capture humans being so exquisitely human, I made some films of that enquiry. I wrote, I talked, I made sure that everyone who mattered knew what I was up to. I would give the surgery a realistic amount of time to assess if it had either improved matters, had not made any difference, or the third unthinkable risk of having the surgery, made it worse. I wasn't willing to stay in this world in the event of either of the last two outcomes. Simple as that.

I showed up at Charing Cross Hospital on February 20th 2020, with my best buddy beside me. I was admitted, gowned, socked, tagged, given indescribable underwear, and then we sat and waited. And waited.

An air of anxiety pervaded the waiting space. A few people were wheeled off to theatre, but certainly not at an encouraging rate. A few whispers hinted that there were equipment problems. Having been told I would be first or second on my surgeon's list, I started to fray round the edges, not least because I could neither sit nor stand for very long without pain escalating to the eat-your-arm-off pitch. After seven hours, we were invited into a side room and told by an utterly distraught nurse that my surgery had been cancelled owing to a lack of the required equipment.

My surgeon came upstairs and we stared into the face of mutual helplessness. There wasn't enough basic equipment. Every day surgeons and their teams fight over who gets what. He needed an X-ray machine for three hours to do my operation. He lost the fight to get it and now it was too late. He said he could book me in for March (he only came into the NHS once a month) but couldn't promise it wouldn't happen again.

I had been hanging by a thread, maybe a few threads, as Leonard Cohen would say, threads of prayers. I had cultivated a direct relationship with my surgeon's PA. I had used my skills to make myself real to her. I had got a date as a result of that. I spent almost three months preparing my post-surgical sabbatical and recovery time, making arrangements with clients, making sure I had budgeted enough funds. It was a task, and I had done it well.

When I found myself back in my own bed that evening, rather than the post-surgical ward at Charing Cross Hospital, I was broken. I knew that I couldn't hang on to those threads any longer. I couldn't undo all that preparation and planning and cancel my sabbatical, invite my work back in and carry on in the void of helpless not knowing.

Leonard The Dog was hurriedly retrieved from where he was staying for the now redundant hospital days. I cried and cried. I took pain meds and sleeping meds and woke up the following morning with *ask for help* the only clear thing I could hear in the echo chamber of myself.

Within 30 hours, I had been given enough money to call my surgeon and book my spinal fusion for February 25th at his private clinic in Harley Street. He was utterly astonished and kept saying: *Your followers must really love you.* I don't have followers. I have friends, community, both heart and blood family. My asking-for-help was shared across Facebook and amongst friends. People I knew deeply, friends of friends, people who read me, and absolute, complete strangers gave me money.

It was overwhelming.

Some suggested I make an actual crowdfunder. I knew that missed the point. I just wrote a letter. It was 853 words. I said that I needed help – that I needed money. I said why. It was a no-frills letter. I said No expectation. No pressure. No manipulation. I said I don't know how to ask like this, and this is me winging it. I said – Thank you for reading me, and that I'd appreciate it very much if this was sent on in any which way that felt right. Or not. It was humble, but without shame.

When I look back at what and how I wrote the letter, I don't quite understand the gift that dropped me below shame and anxiety, and then allowed my heart to speak. It happened though. It was a letter from the simplicity of my heart.

A blessing so far outside my capacity for words – an almost indescribable triumph of human kindness and generosity. My bank and PayPal accounts were flooded with deposits, many from names I didn't recognise. I found two back-to-back transfers, one for £3 and the next for £3,000. I did not know either donor.

Asking and receiving so much has healed something so far down in my baby bones that I am forever changed.

I had the very best version of the surgery I needed. My surgeon said bluntly that he could not have given me this quality of work without the benefit of his own state-of- the-art equipment in his own operating theatre, with a specialist team, and no time pressure. He said the NHS version would have been a Band-Aid at best and could quite possibly have left me in more pain.

Fifteen months later.

A few light bulbs have blown up the biggest blind spot of my little life.

I still live with constant and chronic pain, but it is much less. I can live with it, *living* being the critical word. It is not the loudest thing, though sometimes it is, and it is not the only thing.

It is only now that I can recognise just how little hope I had in the surgery improving matters enough to carry on. I wasn't expecting to still be here. As some of you know, having been kind enough to read me, I hold a clear position on my choice not to get what I call old-old. At some point, I will be done. I will know when I am, and I'll let people know, take care of things, and only wish we lived in a society that would allow me to have a goodbye gathering and create a ritual that walked me to the border of breath. Nevertheless, it will be a riff on that, a departure that doesn't implicate anyone legally. It is only now that I can feel the difference between a choice made because the alternative is untenable, and a choice made in the simplicity of just being done.

This is a chapter of life I didn't expect to have.
The quality of such a space is sinking in – I am sinking into it.
This book is a bow to the strangeness and mystery of still being here.

In the tiny corner where hope hid out, my vision of life improved by surgery and having more time bears little resemblance to where I find myself now. I had imagined a kind of rolling back to a point where, even though I lived in chronic pain, it was manageable and I did more stuff. Going in and out, round and about kind of stuff. My kind of stuff. Dancing, cooking, visiting friends, walking, talking, being able to say *Yes* instead of almost always *No*.

Of course, we don't roll backwards, only forwards. I was nearly sixty-three not forty-seven. The blind spot I mentioned, somehow, I had not understood something so obvious and so basic I can hardly believe myself. It makes me laugh and cry, given the simplicity of falling into what was always here. I believe we wait for ourselves, and maybe we get home, partially home, nearly home. Maybe we don't. Maybe we live and die in homelessness. So much of my life

I have been homeless, searching, seeking and longing for a sense of place.

Leonard Cohen said – *Angels are other people.* Sartre said – *Other people are hell.* I suspect it is all true. When I bow to all my help, some of it has been ugly, some of it hardcore, alongside the tenderness, tenacity, generosity. Some of you out there know you have and do help me, and some people have no idea who I am and have helped me just by being themselves the way that they are or were.

The circle of repetition does not escape me. That I stood in the doorway between living and dying aged 30; and then, another very different 30 years later, I stood in that doorway again. I am still here. I found my way home with the something fierce inside me, alongside all the aforementioned help. When I say home, I don't mean a destination, or a linear pathway. Home in that internal home address sense. Home in the I'm-good-with-the-one-I'm-with-sense. The kind of home that takes a lot of fierce (I think the fierce is longing) and a lot of help, not to mention the willingness to keep allowing what I think I know, am, and will be, fall away. Keep falling away. To keep meeting anew the one I'm with, and to keep meeting others from the simple. Here I am – there you are.

I know the lightness, the weight, the struggle, the sweetness of giving up another little fight, knowing it will come round again, the hilarity to be found in radical simplicity, the freedom and brutality of being awake to what is, hopelessly, imperfectly human, giving up on innocent or guilty.

This life.
This book.
Some postcards.

October 2024
(London, UK)

Déjà vu cards

How Many Miles – Rolling Home, Here I Am

So, my dear friend Rose – editor of this book nudges me to get writing something for Advantages of Age. I say nudge, but it feels more like a poke. A benign poke, but a poke is more staccato than a nudge, and is always a gift. I always say *Yes*, and then I'm writing to some kind of deadline, which serves the writing of the piece.

Maybe boundaries she says, something about boundaries.

Humm, says my mind, mind … *Yes*, says my deeper and quieter voice. Just *Yes*.

I mean, I don't really write self-help, and that's where my mind went. I come from a field of trauma so unspeakable that I didn't know what a boundary was, and I certainly didn't know I had any right to say no to anything. Especially, as it happened, anything sexual. I am a long way down the road from there, and I am in many ways, the more obvious ways, pretty good at saying *No* when required. I have had to say it a lot (too much) over the past three or four years before my back surgery in 2020, because so many simple pleasures became impossible to manage.

In a manner of speaking I teach some of my psychotherapy clients a few bits and bobs about boundaries.

So, the whisper of *Yes*, that this is the thread to pull in the writing, well that's me going down below what I think I know. What I do know, because I don't want to disrespect the effort it has taken to learn about edges and space between, and the beauty and freedom to be found in the simplicity of saying *Yes*, and *No*, and I'm not sure yet, let me think about that.

Underneath, and underneath more, there is a place where I am only a beginner at the slippery business of saying the *No*, that is saying a just born *Yes* to what has been waiting a lifetime to see if I make it.

Yes, I do finally see you there, so utterly alone, so defeated. I finally see the disembodied homeless and hopeless. Me. Caroline the Compassion Queen with all my talk of welcoming and fields of kindness, has only just got to the place where you become visible. I can see you through a vale of tears. I only just made it, and I know there is comedy in this. Tender comedy, tragicomedy. We are all in the soap operas of our little lives, trying to get home before we have to go.

My perspective. It might not be yours.
Remember, I am not in the self-help section.

I didn't know how to listen to my body, though I certainly would have told you I did. I got parts of me home. Dear God, my life has been a pilgrimage, and the many homecomings have been anchoring, rooting me into this earth, the ground, leading me to a sense of place that isn't defined by violence and self-murder. I found kin along the road. I wasn't alone. I started to see myself in the mirrors of my ragged fellow travellers. The original mirror was argued with, bits of it fell off, shattered, got swept away.

If we lived in delusional Disneyworld, where all was linear and orderly, where we get a psychological fact and that's that, well, we wouldn't be human.

Nothing at all about my post-surgery experience has been as I might have written it. I didn't write it, because I didn't believe I would have a life rolling on for very long post surgery. As many of you know, I had planned to leave – had surgery failed to significantly improve the constant agony that had become my reality. The chaos of my NHS surgery being pulled on the day, the despair, the undefended asking for help, the outpouring of generosity from so many through the asking and the receiving – like an enormous wave of unconditional love that had me five days later in my surgeon's Harley Street clinic receiving the very best version of the spinal fusion that is currently available. All of this brought me here.

Here.
Here, to where I didn't expect to be, so I hadn't written myself in. I'd written myself out. It has been more than strange to turn back towards a life I wasn't expecting, and find it full of fragments of old stories.

I have stopped tapping on my keyboard. Ground to a halt.

I'm looking for a word that captures that first year of afterwards. The one that won't go away, even though I'm pushing hard, is torture. I don't want to say it. Hyperbolic, my critical mind says loudly, but truth be told it is the right word. So much of what and how I understood things started falling away. I probably spent that first year trying to hang on to them. That felt like torture.

With the love of some straight-talking mirrors, you know, my people, my kin, my heart buddies, I started to allow what was already happening. I stopped fighting. Not just like that but I did turn a corner. I turned towards my most homeless, abandoned and separate self, the one that was turned away from at the very first breath, by a mother that could only feel hate, revulsion and horror. I come from that lineage.

Along the highways and byways of slogging onwards, of course I came to learn and understand that I had turned away from myself in that very same way. Yet I had missed the embodied abandonment, until not deciding to take my own life because the NHS couldn't give me what the same surgeon could if I paid him. At that point, I couldn't not meet myself in the unoccupied house of my own ravaged body. The surgeon said my lower discs were dust, that he could sweep away and build structure and architecture. That this would hold me straight for the rest of my life.

I didn't know this then, but only if I got it. Only if I saw the one I turned away from because I didn't know how not to. I couldn't stay with the overwhelming experience of arriving in the world in a tiny body, constantly flooded with sensation, if there was no one there to stay with her. I internalised revulsion and absence. It was all I had to breathe in. I took that into every cell, fibre, blood and baby bone of me. Understanding the absence and revulsion and the marks it left on me, I learned how to stay with much of what wasn't stayed with. I found fields of kindness that caught me when I fell out of the fighting not to be depressed.

I just never, ever noticed that the pain in my body that has been as true and baseline as depression has, is the embodied expression of the same simple, unbearable tragicomedy of my little life. I pushed on through everything, every moment of every day, not listening to a single cry or whimper, not hearing my body pleading for mercy.

Even on the dance floors of redemption and in the kitchens of love, everything always hurt, and hurting got louder and I got deafer, and in the end the discs at the bottom of my spine were dust and I could barely move, and I literally could not continue to stay alive if this was my lot.

Back to the boundaries.

I am surgically repaired enough to revert to pushing through, so I had to turn towards that baby that wasn't stayed with, and ask her to forgive me for the very long wait, and ask her to show me how to listen. I had to stop fighting with ideas about becoming someone better (physically) and appreciate I am here already and that words like limits and capacity are love words, not dirty words. I live with pain. I never thought in my wildest occasional dream that I wouldn't, but I live with pain and that is not all there is of me. That is a very big difference. I manage with medication, prayer, physical and energetic support, disciplined and simple core strength maintenance, but mostly by listening to this 63 year-old body that has been waiting a literal lifetime to be heard.

Attuned.

A word that brings tears to my eyes.
A word that shatters my heart into pieces of tenderness that are unfathomable because they belong in the tiny, helpless, wordless and lonely body of a baby that I can actually feel from the inside.

I don't fancy living many more years. I'm not going to get old, old.

I am here living now, and I am attuned to the SOS from the toil of getting here. I'm listening. The message is singing out its purest note. I will work less. I am saying *No*, and I'm sorry I'm not taking any new clients for the foreseeable future. I am making the work that I've come to love and trust myself in more and more as I land by my own fireside – fewer in numbers. If I don't, I will spend the rest of my life offering too much holding, and spend the space in between recovering rather than just being here.

Here to breathe.
Here to finish my one little book.
Here to see more of the ones I love.
Here to not know what's going to happen next.

Here to yield to this moment over and over until this is the end of being in my forgiving body.

My body will always hurt.

Sometimes that feels overwhelming.
In this moment, really allowing the truth and the grief to be here, I am flooded with something I don't have one single word for. I find myself here more often though and am so very grateful. In the absence of one word, or anything elegant, it's the Everything in This.

I don't often spell this out, but a lifetime of clenching against embodiment has left pain everywhere. It was my back that collapsed, and that has been the doorway to coming home, but everything hurts: head, neck, hands, fingers, shoulders, arms, eyeballs, joints. That's how it rolls, and all of the hurting has been so lonely, and isn't lonely anymore.

I listen, imperfectly, and love, imperfectly, every hurt, every clench, every soften and re-clench and soften. I have given up fighting to be a different me, though sometimes I forget I have, and then I remember again.

Gratitude.
Humility.
Hilarity.

It's all I've got.

A Lament for Sinéad

So many wild waves of emotion crash around in the wake of Sinéad O'Conner's death.

Me too. I feel a lot. I've loved and resonated with all she has offered from the very first album. I mean, her voice, and the way she would give herself fully to delivering those songs to us, no matter if songs were penned by her own hand, or the intimacy with which she would enter into someone else's work.

I loved her for her raw art, her passionate heart, most of all, her politics. I bowed to her courage and enduring integrity.

I saw her several times, always shocked at how tiny she was in the flesh. This bird-like woman with a voice that contained the whole ravaged and beautiful world. I saw her last on December 15th 2014 at a BBC recording of the series *Mastertapes*. She was in discussion with John Wilson about her 2007 album: *Theology*.

I was picked to ask my question submitted some weeks in advance, so was seated at the front, a mere few feet away from the conversation happening between the rather suave John Wilson and Sinéad who was dressed shabby-street rather than shabby-chic.

She had a lot to say about God/Gods, religions, dogma, faith and betrayal, not to mention the music industry, love and loss. Everything made sense, but you needed to be able to attune to her frequency which was fast, and nothing like linear.

As her career had rolled forwards and so many times she had unravelled in the public eye, I had started feeling immensely protective towards her. Sitting so close to her palpable vulnerability in 2014, I remember wondering how her story would end. Now it has. Sinéad is free and she left carnage behind. How could she not? History wants to repeat itself. Lineage is powerful in micro and macro systems, and it takes a small or large revolution to change a storyline.

I notice there's a lot of shouting going down in this early afterwards. It is here I find myself writing from. Her fanbase is disparate, some taking oppositional positions regarding 'their' Sinéad. It must be quite a thing, as an artist, inevitably to some degree to be taken hostage by the people you touch, speak to, the people who actually pay your wages in their commitment and love of your work.

Some of Sinéad's people are pretty strong in their beliefs that she represented their position. There are multiple positions of course, and it has taken me a lifetime to land on the shoreline of everything. Everything is another word for freedom in my book and it sure isn't the road most travelled.

What if 'everything' does away with many entrenched binary constructs, and invites us to see ourselves and each other in a new place, so radically simple it's enough to break all our human hearts open?

What if Sinéad's hostage takers could see across the lines that separate, teach and preach that we are enemies, then notice the common threads are all narratives of sorrow, victimisation, exploitation, betrayal, abuse, trauma and injustice? Sinéad died on the cross a thousand times before she died.

One way or another undefended art gives us – the recipients – pieces of ourselves. Sinéad gave us broken, broken hearted, broken shattered, broken beaten, broken lost, broken alone … trauma drove the car, and she didn't make it home.

It doesn't take a psychotherapist, which I am, just a fellow pilgrim, another human rooted in broken to see that her life was a longing, a seeking, a desperation, for a different home address, and that she kept circling back to where it all began and where it ended.

If I had a gravestone which I won't as I've chosen the dust and ashes option, but if I did, it would say: Broken & Whole – In Good Company.

I was leaning into the deep and enduring space with my therapist (who actually isn't a therapist on paper, but she's mine) this morning, letting my sad be really sad, moving right up close and closer to my sad. I said – sighing - *it's good to be so sad*. We laughed while I wept, because we share a sense of divine comedy and tragedy, that the radical simplicity of what is, the everything, is such a big ask.

It asks us to keep giving up the fight, to keep letting what we think we know fall away, to fall into our own loving arms, the ones that have waited , not knowing if we'd ever make it. I was laughing and crying because I did make it home. This is my success story. Making it to the one I'm with and trusting enough to really fall because there is a certain point beyond which there is no return. Yep, we can drift off for a bit, go a tad bonkers, but Home is not negotiable, and it doesn't have a lot of truck for too much fucking about. Come on Caro, calls the heart and boots voice, there is absolutely nothing that's a problem to be solved. It is just this. Always, just THIS, however much some part doesn't want this.

There's a well-loved story, familiar to all those that loved and knew the work of Mr. L. Cohen for the doorway he was, about a time when Mr. C was in the deep suffering of resistance, and his almost life-long spiritual teacher, Roshi told him: *More sad, Leonard, do more sad*.

My sad today, and often nearby, is the grief of what it has taken to get to the weird and wonder of something like freedom. The freedom from seeking what was always already here.

I grieve and grief is holy water.
My sad isn't lonely any more.
I wouldn't change a thing about the toiling, because how could I? This is my little life, and who could I possibly be, or be with if it wasn't just this?
I lament for Sinéad, for the gift of her broken, the lonely of her sad.
I lament for all the fighting about who she belonged to, and who suffered most.

I lament for this world in so many ways, and in my work that is now as it always wanted to be, but couldn't be until it could, I offer the humans that find their way to me my capacity to be safe, and my willingness to not know, to notice what already knows the way and is trying to happen.

I felt called to write a few lines inspired by Sinéad's life and death because she touched me deeply, and I hated the way she was thrown around as a topic of ridicule and judgement. Or appropriated for a cause, toppled, trampled, and shamed, which I suspect she carried quite enough of in her own blood and bones. Of course, she left us her body of work, which is a legacy free of – though threaded through with her lonely struggles and the many cracks where the light flooded in.

Thing is, if she wasn't blessed with her voice and creativity, if she'd been Sinéad O'Connor the ordinary person, her life would have played out the same way. Her life is many lives, especially of women, though not exclusively. Lives of excruciating trauma repetition in regard to attachment (a psychotherapist's) word for love and connection.

I look at this world I am threaded into, a tiny speck in it all and feel lost. I feel my own lineage of lost as well as the thunder and whispers of shared lost. Down below the realms of mind, intellect, even the fluency of my own heart all I can do is yield. I yield to the longing and insistence of my own little life to find its way. The more I yield, the more I can trust being lost, and in many ways the more part of, and separate from, feel true.

I believe the micro lost informs the collective lost, and the other way around, so we are circling into the void. There is so much pain, and so much longing. This seems simple. Pain of separation and longing for connection.

I'm no politician, so I work with the micro systems, being in service to individuals, couples, and small groups, helping the turn towards ourselves to find home ground, in which we are free to be who we truly are, and offer that, however it rolls for each of us, to the bigger kin.

Almost everything we built will tell us – if we are vulnerable, that we are not okay, and should be striving to succeed in being okay. There is a destination culture that kills our capacity to just be HERE.

What if Sinéad O'Conner, the human with an amazing heart and the voice, and the poetry of a river running true, knew in her bones she was always okay, because not okay was redundant? What if the pain of not okay and the violence of her lineage in the context of this world of violent mirrors didn't kill her? What if so much suffering and dying that doesn't make a media storm and goes unseen unless you work in social services, mental health, frontline crisis response, or are just a human with an open heart and eyes, didn't need to keep rolling, gathering momentum? I literally don't know how to end this cluster of questions, having sat gazing at the keyboard and it coming up empty. I'll stand in my boots and heart. There are some tears in my eyes. I'll say: *What if, from the chamber of my own longing and the realism of everything?*

As those kind enough to read my scribbled life already know, I am passionate about death on multiple levels. I don't know anything. How could I/anyone, but personally I long for gone-ness, for the mysterious unfathomable idea of nothing. Whatever it is or isn't, I do trust that the suffering of Sinéad O'Connor is done.

I know she can't hear me, but I thank her for her life, for surviving, for keeping intact the part of her that could make beauty out of suffering and the streams of light that flow through the cracks.

Gratitude and love is all I've got to say when all else has fallen away. Thank you, Sinéad.

Salutations & Love, Mr. L. Cohen

I stand here in the world without you in it anymore, still reeling from America having put Donald Trump in the White House. When I heard that you'd died on the 7th not the 10th, I couldn't help smiling at your impeccable comic timing. Thank you for your last joke.

I could just write:

Dear Leonard,
I thank you.
Love
Caroline

It would, in essence, be saying everything. And yet I do want to add my little voice to the prayers of thanks. A little square in the patchwork or a thread in the weave. So many voices saying thank you.

I received many messages when the world heard you'd died. I found out that way, waking up to the pinging of text messages from beloved friends. Many precious people told me I was their first thought on hearing the news that you had gone.

I am more touched by this than I can say. The truth is, you can't really see me without seeing how you live in my bones and blood. I first found your work when I was incarcerated in a psychiatric hospital aged 13. I can't remember how or why; I had in my possession a small plastic record player and three LPs: *Songs Of Leonard Cohen*, *Songs of Love & Hate*, and Melanie's *Candles in the Rain*.

They were desperate times. I was preoccupied with suicidal thoughts, but could not carry them through. Something was holding me in the world and I couldn't bear to be so held. I was angry, frightened and more horrifyingly alone than I had any vocabulary for. You had the words that pierced my soul. I didn't need to understand all the narrative threads and themes, which I didn't, but I found an echo of the places I was utterly broken, inside your poetry and inside your voice. You became the thread of some prayer, holding me in this world.

It hasn't been a breeze. I've wasted a lot time fighting with depression, from the complete denial of having any such thing, to the final battles of defence against the truth of having the baseline kind. Surely, I could have some super ups to counter the weight of down?

About the same time as you were reporting your depression was gently slipping out of you, I was finally, after all else had failed, learning to welcome mine. I was discovering the taproot of my own tenderness and you, as ever, were helping me. I have loved you for your exquisite writing, for the particulars of your dear voice, for your grace and humanity, not to mention your wicked sense of humour. But, maybe above all else, I have loved you for your tenderness to the human condition and your compassion for our small endeavours. It is through your body of work that I have come to understand I am both broken and I am whole.

I know you needed to come back out on the road for financial reasons, but the fact you kept circling the world, long after your bank balance was restored, was something else. That last, grand tour, in several chapters over some years: well, I hope it was as good for you as it was for us. What a privilege to have been at a handful of those shows. I saw you in London, Brighton, Madrid, Florence and Ghent. I heard you say, more than once: *Friends, I don't know when we'll meet again – but tonight we're going to give you everything we've got.*

Oh my, how you did. And how much gratitude flowed between the audiences and the stage? And, up on the stage too, as you kneeled before your musicians and bowed and bowed again. We were all thanking each other, from the ravaged and beautiful heartland of intimacy. You sure could make an intimate thing happen in a jam-packed auditorium.

In 2013, I got to meet you in a hotel bar. I was waiting to check in and when I looked up you were sitting a few feet away. I did not think or look before I leapt. As I arrived at your chair, I realised in an almost imperceptible micro beat, that I was intruding. It was too late though, and to be honest, I can't be too sorry. I got to see you, upon my request to shake your hand, bring yourself fully into presence. No going through the motions, or a half-hearted, tired gesture for the zillionth fan. You called yourself to attention stood up and took my hand in both of yours. You looked at me properly, like that was your only concern in that moment, and graciously received my gratitude for such good company along the sometimes-treacherous highways and byways of life. *Thank you, my dear*, you said, in your achingly, familiar voice.

A year later in the summer of 2014, whilst enduring a rather desperate day in my little life, I felt compelled to make you a video letter. This was a dreamlike experience, as I recalled afterwards. The evidence remains though, and my rough, technically speaking, badly made film went out into the world via YouTube. It wasn't until several months later that I realised you had seen it. I came upon your note to me on Allan Showalter's website. To know that you took the time, about six minutes in fact, to take me in and receive my love and gratitude, makes me smile. Your response too.

Dear Caroline,
Deeply touched.
More than I can say here.
Thank you.
Love and Blessings,
Leonard.

I wasn't too surprised to hear of your death. Even though you had been perfectly discreet about the details of your illness, it seemed you were near the edge of this world. Your beautiful love letter to Marianne was both cryptic and explicit. Your last album: a love letter and a goodbye if I ever heard one.

I have wondered on occasion how it has been for you, to be so loved, by us, the recipients of your blessed work. As your son, Adam, wrote a few days ago – *Your hand forged tower of work*. You are renowned for your kindness to fans. Friends, as you called us. The paradox of your deep privacy, offset against the naked offering of yourself through the work. You spoke very directly to your people through that doorway. You were such a doorway for me.

Some people have attributed you with godlike qualities. I'm not so comfortable with worshipping my fellow travellers, being by nature more of a love-and-respect sort of girl. I don't think you liked that kind of adulation much, but regardless, it always seemed to me you were so very human. I think you touched so much in so many, just because you gave sublime poetry to the most universal of human dilemmas. You gave us ourselves. You showed us we are luminous as we stumble along, doing our best and doing our worst. Thank you for your life, and for the discipline and devotion to your craft that is the architecture of that *Tower of Song*.

In some ways, I haven't managed much constancy in my life. Not until more recently anyway, as I have found my way to *The Fields of Kindness*. You, though, have been a constant. You have been with me all the way from that corridor floor at the psychiatric hospital. Sometimes I can hardly believe that little girl made it and is now walking towards 60. I wouldn't have made it without you. I mean that most sincerely, Mr. Cohen. I hear your songs and poetry, even when I am not listening to a device or reading a book. You have infused my life with light by showing me how to include and even celebrate the wretched and the wrecked.

The light does indeed come in through what's broken and sometimes the only word on my tongue is, Hallelujah.

Grenfell

I needed to go and see this.

I went to the Serpentine.
I sat under a tree looking through the foliage at the river, eating the biggest and most sublime pain au raisin I have ever seen or had in my mouth. Then I walk slowly to the gallery in the misty rain.

What can I say?
I wish every human would walk through what Steve McQueen made.
It is, in his words, a Remembering.
The film runs for 24 minutes. First you wait together outside the small theatre space.
An empty white room full of light.
People come in, most in pairs or small groups – a handful alone.
We sit and wait to be shown in.

I look around and wonder what brought each person here.
They open the doors and maybe 70 people walk into the small, simple space, with rows of bleacher-type seating, carpeted floor space in front.
A woman asks if anyone needs a chair.
A little more silence in front of a big empty screen.

The lights drop and we see what Steve McQueen's steady camera sees from his helicopter as it flies across green fields, outer suburbs, and then over the London as we know it.

It is on a straight trajectory to Grenfell Tower.

When it gets to the blackened tower, he slowly circles what is there. Many slow circles. He shows us the gutted interior of homes where human lives happened, where men, women, children and animals died. We see some forensic, white-suited up-moving bodies. We see where the cladding burned.

He stops.
He holds his camera in the stillness of it.

The film ends.

No titles.
No credits.
No narration.
No sound track.
The only sound we hear is the helicopter at the beginning and the end, and distant London, very muted.

The woman who offered a chair, now offers transitional space. She says, take your time.

Most people get up and go.
A few stay for a breath or two.
I sit on my front row bleacher, dead centre to the screen, feeling everything and breathing.
I realise it's only me left.
I stand up and bow.
I say out loud: *Thank You, Steve McQueen*.

Outside we are in another white room with a wall containing every name of every human that died in that inferno.

As I have a very bad sense of direction, when I moved through that room, heading I thought for the exit, I was puzzled to find a man asking me to wait a few minutes more, only to realise I'd circled back to the gateway to the film.
I said I wasn't ready to see it again and got sweetly redirected back outside into the misty rain.

The motivation for making it was Remembering.
To make a record before it was disappeared, wrapped up in a clean inoffensive covering so we don't have to see.

Unbearable that the cladding itself was Kensington & Chelsea wrapping up the more obvious social housing look in an effort to be less "offensive" to the elite neighbourhood.

If you can bear it, I encourage you to go and remember for all that can't, or even those that won't.

Racism & Dog Poo: a reflection on hate

For the past eight years, I've been doing a just-before-bed poo-walk with Leonard, my dog. I'm in my PJs smelling of toothpaste. There is the short circuit, the medium and the long. I cross my fingers for the short. It goes how it goes.

I make a practice out of saying good evening to everyone I encounter. Over the course of the first years, I succeeded in making myself visible to the kids that congregate at the top of my road. They are doing their thing, posturing and posing, drinking, smoking weed, doing a bit of dealing. I am an early-old white woman with a dog and a coat over pyjamas. They are unconsciously/semiconsciously disappearing me.

I choose as a quiet act of rebellion against separation – to show that I see them, and invite them to see me. Initially my simple 'good evenings' caused flummox. People like me weren't supposed to acknowledge people like them.

Over time flummox moved through hostility, suspicion and sniggering. One evening someone mumbled something like *Hey*. Slowly but surely, they engaged in this small human contact. Sometimes I now get a *Hey* before I've offered up my good evening. A very stoned young man once said he liked my dog. Me too, I said, his name is Leonard. Thereafter occasionally someone says, *Hey, Leonard.*

This little endeavour to see and be seen makes me happy.

But I also notice how many people respond to my good evening with a violent gaze. It is intense on the receiving end. Many of these people are my neighbours, and when I greet them during daytime, I get ignored, but not a face off of hate.

I know what it's about though I'm curious how the day/night dimensional shift happens.

In my street, around my block, lots of people don't pick up their dog poo. Ergo, there is a lot of dog shit. I know this blanking, and then a more sinister version of it when day becomes evening/night, is me being disappeared as human kin, and seen (not seen) as a demographic to hate for all the dog shit on the street.

I think about hate and separation.

My heart hurts from the state of our beautiful and ravaged world. I gaze unflinchingly at what is, and am in an ongoing practice of maintaining heartbroken/scared/furious/helpless, without being destroyed, devoured or disassociated.

As Kae Tempest says in *People's Faces*: And yes, our children are brave But their mission is vague.
I know I won't be here to see the unthinkable, that is in my humble opinion just up ahead, close enough to touch, and I know there are amazing communities of young activists across our global family. Nevertheless, the power in the majority has the tightest grip on the most terrifying governance.

As Leonard (the man, not the dog) threaded into one of his songs: *There's a mighty judgement coming down*.

My poo walks in this micro experience of being for fleeting moments in the direct gaze of blind hate, take me to thinking about racism. In the beginning, I would take a poo bag and wave it ostentatiously about, like a flag saying: *Look I'm not one of those ones*.

I got to thinking about what if I were a young black man, wearing the ubiquitous hoody, just walking from A to B. I couldn't wave anything about to signify my humanity, that it was safe to see me; that we were two human beings passing on the highways and byways of our human lives.

I put the poo bag back in my pocket.

I'm 65 this autumn. I've seen things change – laws, culture, attitude, vocabulary – and I'm grateful for the movement around these terrible oppressive norms. However, I'm not convinced it is more than a surface change. The kind of change that matters only comes when we dig deeply collectively and face into our own carried-for-generations legacies of separation, judgement, hatred and violence.

We have hate-crime legislation.
There was a black president in the US.

We have built equality into our systems, and yet at the same time we had Donald Trump in the White House, police killing black boys and men on film on phones, and women being raped and murdered by people in positions of trust and accountability.

At this point in the UK, I find the difference between Labour and Conservative difficult to distinguish. I'm ambivalent about my Labour Party membership, although I rate my local MP very highly.

Politics spin the line about how we all matter, while the clear demarcation between those that have value and those that don't is so massive a chasm that social justice and equality is way out over the horizon, forever I believe out of sight.

The hard-won abortion legislation that gave women choice and agency has been revoked after 50 years in the US. And there is talk about it here.

Personally, I am very grateful to the Internet in general and social media, though I am a total dinosaur, and only use Facebook, and very recently, sometimes Instagram. I love it for its doorways to contact, intimacy, knowledge, relationship, shopping without going to shops! Oh my, I hate shops (mostly) with occasional exceptions.

I love it for everything it gives me, which, except the convenience stuff, could be distilled into one word: connection.

I know though that it has the darkest underbelly.
It has highjacked so many of our children (and adults).
It has (in my humble opinion) destroyed democracy.
It is teaching the young everything that is counter intuitive to deeply intimate erotic joy.

It is a gateway to so many different shapes and flavours of violence, and it is used ruthlessly to destroy so much that matters so much.

Social media is used to target, manipulate and teach hate and separation. We are being played without even noticing. Everything that has always been in the fields of human dynamics and complicated is now on steroids.

I don't get any rabid right-wing promo because all the algorithms know I'm neither leaning that way, or lost and susceptible. I get a reflection back of who I already know I am – showing up on my feeds.

We are being taught, both overtly and more worryingly less obviously, to see any kind of difference as the enemy. The only thing that brings us together, to the place where the simple truth that we are all kin underneath our costumes, skin colour, sexual orientation, gender, ways of living life, rituals, churches, no church, neurodiversity, beliefs, is to keep seeing one another across the differences and be open to recognise the humanity that threads us together. We are all in it together, like it or not.

I have community, intimate friendship, a hard won compassionate and loving relationship with the one I'm with, having nearly succeeded in destroying myself through the pain of coming into this world via a micro lineage of revulsion and hate.

I occupy the places where connection and authenticity are the paramount cultures and though I am rather solitary, I am connected, seen and loved by the wideness and closeness of my heart Familia. I am home.

To be able to say that as I walk towards the end of everything – fully aware old – that old age is not for me, is my success story. (My tongue is jammed in my cheek as I do not believe in any kind of binary success and failure construction.)

Yet it does matter that I got home which wasn't looking likely on paper.

Home means I feel the pain of what has become of us, the big us, as I cherish the home ground of community, connection with self, others and the natural beauty of our planet as it gets murdered breath by breath.

Grief runs through me like a clear, cold alpine stream. It knows the way.

I am also discovering that underneath the fields of kindness and simplicity there is another place. I'm not sure peace is exactly the right word, but it is a kind of peace. Not the classic body of beautiful still water but full of movement, full of everything – it is everything.

It's the quality of the everything that has opened and yielded. If it had a voice, it would be whispering, over and over: *Yes this, yes this too, yes this*. This is a new place for me and to go back to Kae Tempest again: "Even when I'm weak and I'm breaking I stand weeping at the train station, 'cause I can see your faces. I love people's faces".

The faces I meet on my evening poo walks are always going to take me for a moment to the impossible question of – what if I was walking this life in a black male body. I'm glad it takes me there. Sometimes I have an impulse to stop a neighbour on the road, and ask: *What are you feeling? Who are you seeing?*

I might even do that some time. If I do, no doubt I'll write about it.

I live between being ripped to shreds and finding so much peace in people's faces.

The Wolves of North-West London

This is a small tale; it might be somewhat true and other-what imagined.
Some people may be lightly disguised to protect their privacy and/or sensibilities.

I am, however appearing as my true self.
I'm that line in the rolling credits that mostly people don't bother watching, where it might read something like:

Jon Snow – Himself.

Caroline Bobby – Herself.

I'm having fun.
Enjoying a simple pleasure.

There's a community market down my street, next to the Farmer's Market. It comprises a series of stalls selling nice, sometimes exquisite stuff, that is often but not always overpriced.

There's a website and everyone's 'whatever it is' has a name, identity and a little bit of blurb to say what's what.

All except one that is.
Anty's stall doesn't have a name, and it's not on the website.

I don't even know if it's Anty, Annty, or it could hilariously be Anti.

Anty's stall sells all sorts of things. New things. Everything from cosmetics, through jewellery, amazingly diverse ceramics, bags, some clothes, purses, gorgeous notebooks and pads, kitchen stuff, utensils, pots, dishes … I really could keep going and this would become more an epic list than a story.

There's a particular face moisturiser that I love.
I love that it's a staple and constant product that Anty just always has. She sells it for half the recommended retail price, meaning I can afford to use it as my regular face cream.

Over the years of buying cream, and more than occasionally beautiful dishes, bowls, and micro bowls. Who can have too many tiny vessels for tiny things? I also give them to people I love.

Over these years I have had the added pleasure of slowly noticing that Anty is a natural, subversive comic. She has a whole repertoire of non-verbal commentary, that is so understated I have sometimes wondered if she's fully conscious of the fun she's having with herself at some level.

You see, Anty's stall is catnip or cocaine to the Wolves of my little corner of London. She is stormed by mostly a particular demographic. Not entirely. I don't like to generalise, and besides I'm there too.

It's the storming that makes my belly laugh.
There is devotion involved. Congregating happening before the market opens its doors, and when they do open there's an

animalistic, somewhat ruthless wave of intent, heading straight for Anty.

She always has two or three young girls on the cusp of becoming young women along for assistance. I used to wonder if these were daughters, and asked one once. Apparently not. Anty doesn't seem to be anybody's mother, at least not in this constellation.

This leads me down a pathway of whimsy. I imagine Anty has a hybrid place of education and these girls and others, are students. It is part Hogwarts, part this-life feminist, part circus school, and a hundred percent 'one for all, and all for one'.

In other words, I'm dreaming up the community, village, home ground that I needed at that age, and was so far away from. Probably Anty does have kids and these are friends or cousins that need weekend work.

Whatever the real story is, they are a pretty skilful team. As the wolves crowd around, and a bit of snarling, biting and bleeding goes down, they take it with fluidity: like a rushing river that knows the way.

One day, I get a possible association to her name. She appears wearing a most beautifully weathered sweatshirt; once black, now soft, worn, more charcoal than black. I just know she has lived and loved in this garment over a long time and wonder how old she was when she acquired it, what the story is.

There are fading, once white words across the front.
They read: I am an Antelope.

I think: did your parents christen you Antelope, and now you're Anty for short? I quickly notice what a car crash of assumptions are in that line of wondering, but oh how that shirt tickles me, and I feel ridiculously delighted whenever she wears it.

About a year ago Anty's stall suddenly got significantly smaller. We'd become lightly chatty by this time, so I asked what was going on.

She reported that she was tired of working so hard and maybe moving in the direction of retirement.

Of course, I'm totally on board with this from my human, empathic part … I talk about the art of resting, pausing, leaning in, putting a weary head down. She tells me she's not good at any of that, and I tell her it's a learnable skill.

My more self-serving part is concerned about her face cream dealer disappearing off the block. I notch up the product purchasing, much less casual now I have learned that Anty is practising, in theory anyway, the art of resting. Having once been a 'buy some when I'm there, not to worry if it's all gone by the time I hit the market', sort of shopper, I have now become a Wolf. I arrive 10 minutes before the doors to the hall are opened. I lurk, trying to look like I'm not contriving to position myself nearest the door so that when they open I can move briskly, but not actually gallop like a beast after prey.

I've located the market manager and got the inside track on which weeks Anty has booked her stall, as she no longer comes every time, which is I'm guessing in sympatico with her working less project.

I'm also noticing that I'm actually stock piling these iconic blue glass jars, not so free and easy with giving them out to others as little pressies and treats.

Truth be told I want to make sure I've got enough to see me out. As many of you know, I'm not hanging in for getting old past a certain point. That being done point is closer now, so I probably don't need to worry about running out before I stop breathing, when moisturising my face is no longer a concern.

I really am in already enough land, but I am weird, and can't quite stop being a wolf, just to make sure – and, actually Anty seems to be upsizing again, which leads me to wonder about the rigours of her learning the Art of Resting

I could more than likely soften and settle.
I could step aside a little, go back to the more observational position, but for now there's a little more juice to be squeezed out of being one of the wolves – and never again, even when I'm back in the watching the wolfing going down will I be able to forget that I went there once.

Like any decent visit to another country, "Wolf Country" has changed me. We come back from anywhere we've been, just a little bit different. I notice I am less judgmental, now that I have been and still am a tad, one of the wolves. No longer separate, I can see more clearly that though many don't have an actual need for heavily discounted shopping, what do I really know about fellow humans behind their costumes and artifice?

Because I lurk and I listen, I've heard some astonishing things as shoppers approach and retreat from Anty's vicinity ... Once I saw two women, wildly overdressed and over botoxed, walking away as purposefully as could anyone in such tight skirts and stilettos. They were laden down with several of Anty's eclectic selection of reused bags: anything from Aldi to Harrods, and one said to the other: *Darling woman, that Antigone, she absolutely adores me.*

I told Anty about catching this sometime later and she did one of her marvellous understated snorts.

As for me, well my wolf is going one more time, to the last Christmas market, then having had a chat with myself about the reality of my stockpiled yield, I will hang up my wolf costume and return to wolf watching from the privilege of having been one.

Small stories

Sparrow

She knew that teenagers were supposed to be obsessed, and she was that.

She knew nothing of boys, bands or reality television. She didn't like shopping or alcopops or iPhones. She just didn't care.

She knew she wasn't normal. She was outside, not inside and always had been. Always would be if she had her way.

Her obsession was flesh and lots of it. As things stood, she didn't have much. Her 17-year-old body was spare, lean and angular. She was thinner than thin, less than petite. All her bones were there to see beneath tightly stretched skin. Her breasts didn't exist, and her bottom was flat. She gave up many hours to running dissatisfied hands over her sparrow self.

She dreamed another body, her true body. She watched a TV show once about transsexuals and recognised herself in the boy who said he was truly a girl. She was truly enormous, not sparrow tiny. She dreamed of mountainous flesh, and of being a queen in the very centre of the mountain that was in her heart. She resided within folds and valleys, crevices and caves.

She was a mythical creature of unfathomable proportions. This was her obsession: becoming herself.

She was ready. She had crystallised her visionary longing into an action plan, and despite the odds, she never once considered she would fail.

She had lists and sublists of things to learn about how to get fat. She made goals and timelines and spreadsheets. She painted a picture of where she wanted to be. She is enthroned in a golden room, a goddess, a mountain, a place where people come to worship.

Breathing in and breathing out, the dedicated labour of pushing air through herself.

Just out of definition and focus, in the corner of this picture is the person who will help her. She can't quite see who it is yet. She wonders where she'll find him. She knows it is a boy. Will it be church or the Internet? Or somewhere more prosaic like Sainsbury's or the library?

She needs more money to fund her project.

Maybe her mentor will be rich, probably a man then rather than a boy. Her pillars of papers and possibilities link together and spawn more. She waits until nightfall and creeps into other people's houses. She is small enough to slip through the cracks so doesn't need a lock pick or a rock. She always knows where to find the treasures, and is accumulating a stash that she hides at the back of her wardrobe at home. In all honesty, it doesn't take much to hide from her parents, but treasure needs a special place regardless.

She has to finish all her stage one preparation before she can start getting fat. She can't risk getting too big to go stealing until she has enough, and she can't risk getting big enough to be visible until she has her own Temple. She works hard at night, and during the daylight she looks for her boy or man on the computer. There are not many seeking a position of such particular service and she has not found him yet.

She knows he's out there and that he's looking for her; that they will recognise each other instantly. She is patient on this. For now, she is as happy as she's ever been, tasting new words in her mouth such as joy, pleasure, and homecoming. They taste good. Sometimes she laughs out loud and the hands that run over her body are forgiving because soon she will start to shift her shape. The longest list of all her lists is the one with all the different foods she will eat and eat when she starts stage two. She loves this list and sometimes licks the paper it is written on.

Bebe

She woke up too early this morning. It was dark and hazy cold. The little black panther was racing, leaping, zooming up and down the length of home.

She made a half-asleep decision to open up the cat flap for the first time. A streak of pure joy flew through and out into the cold before dawn.

She went to sleep and dreamed anxious dreams.

When she woke properly at 7am, she stood shivering in the back garden calling to no avail.

Silence happened.

She told herself: it's okay, she's safe, she's a cat, she's having an adventure. She'll be back soon.

Worry escalated.

Please don't be dead.

I'm sorry I let you out so early.

The prayers got louder, and under the noise she knew full well that going to a scheduled writing workshop would be out of the question without Bebe's return.

She saw herself walking the streets, calling and calling, and as she descended into the full spiral vortex of this, Bebe slipped back through the cat door.

Oh, she said, suddenly empty of everything except space, *Thank you for coming home.*

Horses

I dream of horses.

I lay down, close my eyes, and there they are.
It is an ocean; a dream ocean. In real life, I've only ever seen the grey and rainy sea. Only once or twice. I've never been in any waves.

Here, the sky is wide and blue and the sand is white. The ocean is rolling, a symphony of blue hues and greens.
The horses are always waiting for me. They crowd around me, nuzzling, nudging, welcoming.
I kiss salty, velvet noses. I leap. I land like lightness that is not true in real life, up onto the warm wet back of invitation, and as a group of grace and substance, we gallop through the waves.

I am always in the centre.
There are always six.
It is something I don't have any words for.

After a while, these horses relinquish the sand-ground beneath their hooves, and we are swimming, rolling with the waves. I am free.

It is always a horrible shock to find myself back in real life. My horses gone.

I am eleven years old.
I want to die.
My parents tell me I'm a big problem and take me to doctors.
Once I try and tell one of them about the horses. He doesn't understand.
He talks to my parents as if I'm not there, saying things about delusions, disorders, and gives me more pills.

I quite like some of the pills. They make me feel floaty and lighter, and even sometimes smiley. But I always return to horrible, and am given another pill. The doctors say I am acting out. They say if it gets worse, I will have to go to a hospital.

That's what happened.

I got worse. School, which was hell, asks me to leave. It's called being expelled. Neither parent ever says that to me. Years later, when searching for myself in boxes and cupboards in an empty house, I find letters to my parents documenting my expulsion.

It's a weird thing, not knowing what's going on, only that it is all so wrong.

Hospital is hell. I am the only child.
They are giving me so many pills and injections, and when I get angry (that's called acting out) they give me ECT. That's short for Electric Convulsive Therapy.

Here, I can't find the horses.
They don't come.
I want to die.

Shirley Alexander

Shirley Alexander was a guest in my life for a comparatively short period of time. In actuality, it was less than 12 months. She certainly left her mark on me, and in the end, she left me her chair.

It all happened a long time ago. I was 20 years old and I was lost. I was a refugee from a dysfunctional family and an alcoholic mother. I was hopelessly addicted to destruction. I was a junkie for chaos and pain.

Shirley picked me up one night. I was weeping at the train station, drunk and maudlin.

Suddenly, before me was a creature: a woman yes, but palpably both more and less than that. She wiped tears from my eyes with pale fingers, and I knew without any grasp of how I knew, that she had come to help me.

I followed her home without a whisper.

On arriving at a recessed wooden door set into a wall – and almost invisible – she slipped in a key and opened us into somewhere else. It was a distinct experience of a small fall.

I went with it, this small fall. I landed in gardens, naturally curving and rolling, not a sniff of structure and form. I could hear water running and smell the earth. Shirley took my hand and led me towards a large, weathered wooden building. It seemed like it grew out of the ground.

Inside was light, space, big wicker baskets. There were two pieces of furniture; a massive bed in the centre, and not too far away, a chair that I fell in love with in an instant.

I have to tell you that I'd never fallen in love before.

The chair was a big circular cradle, fashioned out of strong blond bamboo cane, and lined with the softest, sunset-coloured cushions and pillows.

Shirley gave me a key, and said: *Come when you need to. You are welcome here.*

I came when my heart and feet brought me.

Healing was happening, though I had no conception of what that meant.

Pieces of me were finding other pieces of me, and slowly I began understanding how lonely I had been for myself. There, but so much separation in ascendancy.

I wasn't so surprised the day I opened the door and found Shirley had gone. The wooden building was full of light and full of Shirley. Everything was gone except the chair and I knew it was a gift for me.

For a while I came back to be with the chair, and with all the feelings I had for Shirley Alexander. When it was time, I took the chair and shut the door behind me for the last time.

The world is ravaged, broken and beautiful.

I sit in Shirley's chair a lot.

It is the place where I always remember how simple it is, how everything and nothing coexist and there is never anywhere to get to.

A Blonde Woman

I'm on a Bakerloo line train. It's loud, clunky and abrasive, and I've disappeared inside myself. I'm in a floaty, abstract geography, not really anywhere in fact.

Gradually, I become aware that I'm aroused. My pussy burns, my chest and throat tighten and my breath catches. Never one to question a wave of erotic pleasure if it comes, I'm practising the fine art of not squirming too obviously on a tube train, when I look up and catch her eye.

Now, if this were a movie queue some wild soundtrack, or some other hot-fuck sound. As it is, I am instantly plugged into, pierced by a fierce, erotic current, turned up full and then some.

I look. I breathe. I see a blonde woman with milky skin sitting opposite. I can't even take her in properly because I'm so turned on. A small part of my brain, of reason, and maybe of fear, tries to get a word in, but I am lost and happy to be so. Whatever this is I give myself up to it. All thought of a lunch meeting with my accountant is thrown to the wind.

The train screams Into Marylebone Station, and she stands up, looks at me with bright, unapologetic eyes. I am on my feet and following her without question. She moves briskly through the people and the space, leading us up and out into daylight. I am consumed by the sight of her shoulders and back, the bounce in her step, and her arse, held softly by faded jeans, slung low on her hips.

As we emerge from the ticket barriers and turn into the hustle and bustle on the pavement I am pushed with utter conviction up against the station wall. I briefly see the eyes of the newspaper vendor behind her widen, and then the only eyes I can see are hers. She stands a little taller than I and gazes down into my face. Her hands catch hold of my hip bones, curve round my butt, and she pushes her hips and lower body hard between my legs. I am panting on Marylebone High Street.

Up against my pussy and clit I can feel a straining erect cock. My mind folds over and I'm trying to compute what I feel. This wonderful creature must be running round town with an amazing strap-on under her jeans. And while this makes logical sense. I know this is no dildo. I am feeling a real live cock. I know I am. As she rocks and rolls her cock, yes, her cock, with absolute precision through her jeans and my jeans, into the crack between my legs, pushing under, up and over my swollen clit, I feel myself start to orgasm. She feels me break open and kisses me deeply and sweetly. She sucks my tongue and holds me up against the wall as I ride the waves and feel tears rush to my eyes.

I am upright and walking. She has hooked me tight against the side of her body with her arm. It's a good fit and we walk together like one animal. She ducks and swirls and spins through the people like a top, and stops outside a blue door in a back street. She produces keys from her front pocket, unlocks and opens up. It looks like a car park staircase inside and she pushes me upwards. Suddenly we are both laughing and rushing up the stairs, two at a time. Breathless. Urgent. At the top, there is another door and another key and we crash into a new space. It feels very different and I have a sense of light and watery colours. I want to look more and yet all of me is utterly attuned to this woman who is handling me.

She holds my shoulders, the length of her strong arms between us. We take each other in, both of us breathing hard. She is gorgeous, blonde, slim, absolutely lush. I can see the rise and fall of her creamy breasts, encased in the thinnest of silk shirts, top buttons open, and otherwise moulded to her curves like the silk is her skin. I look down and see how her button-up denim sits low on her hips. A soft black belt is threaded through the loops of her jeans and fastened with a tarnished, silver buckle. My breath quickens as I gaze at the unmistakable bulge of her cock in her pants. She catches my chin and her hand pulls my gaze upward.

Okay lady, she says, *before we go any further and believe me, we will. Before we exchange names or I welcome you into my home in a more orthodox manner. Yes, before any of that happens my lovely, you are going to suck me off.*

She starts to unbuckle her belt, eyes, never leaving mine. I meet her looking, and then succumb to looking down. Her hands are fluent; unbuttoning to expose skin, a blonde, thatch of pubic hair. She pulls open her fly and pushes her pants down over her arse. My heart pounds as her cock emerges hard as a rock and astonishing.

My cunt aches and contracts and a whimper escapes from my mouth. I sink to my knees before her and inhale. I want to smell her cock, her body and her clothes. Her cock is beautiful, big, not enormous, solid, thick and circumcised. I am touching the glistening tip of this glorious cock with my tongue, and this glorious woman, whose name I don't even know, makes a sound deep in her throat. It is partly a moan, also a purr, a growl. I shuffle and crawl closer in and take my tongue and mouth underneath, right into the space between her legs. I take her balls, soft and delicious, heavy like ripe fruit, into my mouth one at a time, and feel her quiver on my tongue. I lick the length of her cock from under and over, follow her on my knees as she falls back a little so the wall supports her. She pushes her hands with rough and tender in equal measure, into my hair and holds my skull like our lives depend on it.

Open your mouth, she says, like a beggar. *Open your mouth for me.*

I do. I kneel before her like a prayer, my mouth stretched open and dripping with a shameless need to be fucked like this. She pulls my face onto her cock. She shakes. We shake together like staccato drumming. She is screaming. I know she's going to blow fast and I want all of her. She's fucking my mouth as I've never been fucked before. Never had so much cock in my mouth, never so deep. She hits the back of my throat over and over and over. Her hands cup my head, and I open totally as her hot gushing spunk blows down my throat. I have no barrier. She convulses and rams in deep and hard. I don't even have to swallow. I am an open channel to receive what pours out of her, into me.

Collapsing into a holy mess. We pant. She licks and kisses my face, pushes her tongue inside my ravaged mouth. Fire rushes through every cell and dust particle, my cunt is sobbing. I am the beggar now.

Please, I whimper.

Please. I lay before her, spreading my legs wider than I thought I could. I pull myself open more. My clit and cunt pulsate, while she watches with such a smile, such delight, such power. She stands and pulls me upright, pulls me fast to a big bed, pushes me hard so

I fall back. She stands above me, moving her pelvis in a shameless rude dance. Her cock thickens and is rock hard in a beat.

Strip, she whispers. *Take everything off for me.*

I scramble out of my tattered clothes and look into her hungry gaze.

Get on the bed, she tells me. *Put some pillows under your arse. Raise yourself up. Close your eyes and breathe. Don't even think about touching yourself. Wait.*

I do as I'm told.

I feel her walk away, and I feel her return. I know she stands over me. I feel her gaze penetrating me as surely as the cock that's coming.

Eyes open, she says gently.

I look up at the most stunning woman ever. She is all woman; except she has cock instead of cunt. Her cock is jumping under my looking, and she spits into her palm, taking hold of herself, slowly fucking her own hand as she moves closer, kneeling in between my wide-open legs, closer and closer until the head and the shaft, the thick and the length of her push into the waiting, the longing, the hunger. I start to orgasm as soon as she enters me. She fucks my orgasm, and when it starts to throw me on the shore of being done, she looks into a place no one's ever been or seen, and fucks me through the done into a new country.

Doctor Bibi

Maria presses Dr Bibi's doorbell on the dot of 7am. She is very precise. Every weekday morning on the dot of seven Maria presses this bell. She wears an expensive and super accurate wristwatch and is therefore able to be absolutely certain that it is indeed the dot of 7am when she touches her finger to the bell.

This particular morning is a Wednesday in June, and it is Maria's fourth year of this 7am ritual.

As always, the door is released from the inside, and Maria crosses the threshold. She walks easily from one dimension into another. She leaves behind the familiar geography of her journey; 25 minutes on foot from one front door to the other. She leaves behind the order of things on the outside, which is considerable. She steps from one story of herself into Dr Bibi's hallway.

It is easy now to make this move, though it hasn't always been so. In the beginning, the transition from outside to inside had made Maria shake. She would find herself, day after day, trying desperately not to vomit all over Dr Bibi's hall carpet. She would find herself trying desperately to breathe, trying much too hard to quieten her thumping heart. She was trying to stay alive, to arrive inside the room with Dr Bibi and lay her body back into the comfortable thing she had not understood until relatively recently, feeling held. She loves this new grasp – feeling it rather than thinking about it.

In the beginning she couldn't even see what she was walking through or arriving into. Her super sharp eyes failed her and the physical space itself was dark and hostile. Now she can see where she is; see and feel the texture, the energy field of Dr Bibi's space. See and walk into Dr Bibi's somewhat old-fashioned taste and style. She feels it like enfoldment.

Now the hallway is a softer place; a different kind of transitional space.
Sometimes it is a long walk down the hall, and sometimes very short. Sometimes the structure of the hallway stays solid and still, and on other occasions, everything rolls and rocks around, beneath and above her.

These are the mornings that frighten her a lot. This fear takes her far away from the parts of her that have a story of sorts. There is a whisper that Dr Bibi seems able to hear even as she spins into a vortex where there are no words at all. Everything that happens there is overwhelming. Her body floods with everything and a desert of empty.

The Boy

I thought you knew, I whispered. *I really thought you knew.*

How the fuck would I know? He started to cry, and it was victim, whimpering, kicked animal crying. It made me hate him.

Well, you must've chosen at some level not to know. I could hear the ring of moral high ground and so could he.

Don't get all psychotherapist with me, he shouted.

It's not helpful to shout.

And I suppose it's not appropriate either, he carried on shouting.

We were standing up now. Facing off. Standing off. *You should've told me – that's what might have been fucking helpful.*

What am I supposed to do with that?

He looked ridiculous. A little boy and a man all rolled into one.

Fuck you, he said sniffing.

Fuck you too, I said, hating myself and him.

I walked into the kitchen.

Wine? I yelled over my shoulder.

Beer, he muttered.

I got him a bottle and slugged mediocre white wine into a huge glass.

When I returned to the other room, he'd sorted his face out and looked like himself again. We locked eyes across the distance we'd created.

Shall we have sex? He said, in too small a voice.

Not a chance, I said. **Fuck off home.**

Sam

It's time to go home.

I sigh, stretch and roll my shoulders, pulling myself up to full height, and release the stress of postering and posing. It's a regular little routine I do outside the fire station, and it takes it out of me, as much as all that sex in cars.

It's almost 6am and above me the sky is cracked with pink and orange light. I breathe it in. I am walking my familiar way down Darlinghurst Road, through the early morning debris of Sydney's Kings Cross and I am breathing in this amazing light. I do it every morning after work. It's a meditation. Not that I've ever done a class or learned a chant or a mantra, or even wanted to. I've not read much about such matters. I just know I need to anchor myself into earth, and small rituals help steady and settling happen.

This work I do can shake people a long way from steady.
We (that's Sam and me) made a contract with the spirits to keep ourselves steady. It's not for the faint-hearted, such a contract. Sex work and opiates have a way of bringing the best of us to our knees.

I am on my way home.

Stopping at the store for provisions, I'm gathering the makings of breakfast to take home to Sam. Avocado, Italian bread, Parma ham, a luscious sun-ripe mango, and champagne, ice-cold from the fridge.

I get a slippery, wet-mouthed look from the young Greek shopkeeper, a wannabe pimp. I know him. Trying to play a big man on the mean streets. He's pretty much a laughing stock, though he's got a couple of really young girls brand new from the hicks, convinced he's for real. He smacks them about, takes their money and doles out the drugs. Funny thing is, if they make it through initiation, work out the lay of the land, and how to work it, they'll be laughing at him too.

I take my shopping to the till and I smell he's unravelling into a coke crash. He hates me anyway; I give him a fifty and he's off.

You little Bitch, he hisses.
You cunt. You think you can do what you like around here, work for yourself, make your own rules. One of these days someone's going to hurt you, really fuck you up, cunt.

I stare him out. Easy to do, but dangerous as he's so flaky from needing coke. I keep it simple. *Give me my change, call your dealer and get out of my face.* I say it up close and stand solid as a rock.

He hates it that he can't make me shake. *Get out bitch.* He's spitting now with rage. *You're just another fucking, junkie, whore bitch.*

Well, I am indeed, a junkie and a whore. Not nobody's bitch though, except sometimes for an awful lot of money. Outside with my click-clack, fuck-you shoes on the sidewalk, I take great big breaths of dirty air. It doesn't ever do to let the bully boys see they get inside. I never do let them see that. I'm cold and hard and steely on the outside, but sometimes they do get in. Mostly early in the morning, after a long night, after having fucked a lot of men and made a lot of money. And when my drugs are wearing off.

I need to go home.

I always walk home even when I'm really tired. Lots of empty cabs go by, but I like to walk. I've got good strong legs and I like to walk. It's a meditation. Walking home is important because what I'm really doing is walking out of work and into home. I need to feel myself doing that. The sun is coming up and I'm smiling. I can see our house and Sam is inside it waiting for me.

Our house is a secret world, and it's perfect. It's a Sydney house, painted Mediterranean blue and covered at the front in trails of jasmine and frangipani. It smells like heaven at our front door. It's ours. Sam's and mine. We bought it three years ago and we owe no money on it now. All ours. Inside we have made heaven on earth.

I stand on the porch and rest my forehead against the flaky blue wall. I breathe in. I must've made a sound because the door opens and I'm in Sam's arms. Then I know I'm home.

Sweetheart. She smiles at me. Hand in hand we walk to the kitchen. I've put down the shopping and slip out of my click-clack shoes. I'm suddenly four inches shorter. A good height for kissing but we don't. I'm still wearing the tastes, smells and energies of last night's men. You have to have boundaries in this line of work.

We have a routine, a coming home ritual that is Sam's gift to me. She's already done her ablutions. She gets home earlier and washes alone. We both do sex work. She's a dancer. A stripper. So hot, she burns up the men from the suburbs who come back time after time to see her show. She's a legend on the North Shore. She's a five-star tease. No one gets to touch her though. Those are her boundaries. We talked a lot about this, and both know the truth about ourselves. Where we can and can't go. It's made us very honest, sorting it all out. Made us say things out loud that don't generally get spoken. We are unflinching and it makes us work.

Sam is mothering me now. Neither of us had much of a mother to speak of so we give a little to each other in different ways, in different moments. My time to receive is after work. She picks up my shoes and gently guides me into the dressing room. This room is a transitional space, the container for all the trappings of our work. It's an extravaganza in here: leather and lace, satin and silk, underwear that's barely there, stilettos and thigh length boots, latex and lamé, make-up a drag queen would die for. We made it very intense on purpose – very loud and proud – so we always remember what we do for work. Actually, it's a bloody work of art.

Standing, weary now while Sam strips me down. I love this. So familiar. So soft. I drop my head for a moment on her shoulder and I feel held. In this moment she's got all of me. She takes off my corset, unzips my tiny leather skirt, unhooks my suspenders, peels off my stockings and gives me back to myself.

I am naked.

Come on darling, she whispers. We leave the room, closing the door behind us.

The bed and the bathroom are one, with just an open archway set into the dividing wall. It's big and beautiful up here. The place in the house where its heart beats most loudly. It's the Botanical Gardens meets 90's lesbian boudoir. Right now, I'm lying in the bath. Hot, hot, steamy, aromatic, I'm immersed all except for my head.

I have already dunked my head under and my hair is plastered to my skull. Sam says I look like a seal. I'm having a fag. One of the four that I allow myself each day. We are very controlled about our addictions in this family.

Sam is sitting like a shiny, punk angel, using a low wooden blanket box as a table. She is cooking up our drugs. Annie Lennox is singing to us. Our coming home ablutions and using music. I like to watch her. She is precise and reverent about her business.

She knows I like to watch her.
It's part of our erotic dance. It's foreplay. You have to understand that injecting narcotics can be very, very sexy.

Wasn't always like this, mind. In my former life it turned to shit. I was a mess then. Jacking up in public toilets, getting beaten up, ripped off, desperate, unsafe sex with unsafe punters, getting hurt. It was street addict normal.

I was lost out there in Sydney's Kings Cross. Dying. I decided to live and I turned it all around. It was hard work. Not many people down where I was turn it round. Some find their way to a drug rehab, but I didn't want to give up drugs.

Some people get rescued but I'm not that kind of girl. So, I guess you could say that I rescued myself. Now I live a life I like, a life I built against the odds.

I know I couldn't, wouldn't have made it without Sam.

I still whore for a living, but it's different now. I learned to do my job well, not to hurt myself, and how to sniff out when it isn't safe. I still work out of cars, partly because it feels more honest, and I don't want to be anybody's whore but my own.

You won't find me down on the strip being pimped, or working in some man's brothel. I run my own business from opposite the fire station, and I have a good laugh with the boys on the nightshift. They like me, but don't understand why I won't fuck any of them. I have good punters who always come back for more. Like I said, I learned to do my job well, to give a good service, to stay safe and to make a lot of money.

I am still a junkie.
I am still a junkie, and I have reclaimed that word, that label. Lesbian. Junkie. Whore. All mine now.

I turned it round. I turned it round with Sam. It's no mean feat to get on top of a passionate relationship with something as unforgiving as heroin.

We did it though, we do it, we live it, and I have to say we are proud. Not arrogant, just proud. Justly proud.

Sam and I, we have a lot of rules. We never use unless both of us are present, designated times so it is always ritual. We set amounts and always negotiate the increases. We have a monthly budget, buy in bulk from one safe place. Never ever, ever, score off the street.

Keep it clean in other words.
I had a lover, a long time ago – Chris – she always said to keep yourself nice on the outside. She didn't make it. Nodded off while driving her car and died. I guess that's another one; never use and drive. You have to be a control freak to make this work, and Sam and I have raised control to a high art form.

We made a buy this week, and I'm watching Sam measure out from a big bag of white powder. God, it turns me on. I get out of the bath and wrap myself in an aqua coloured sarong. I sit down beside Sam. Now we kiss.

Oh, how we kiss.

I've cleaned my mouth and now it's hers again.

She reclaims her territory and cracks open my heart, head and cunt. *All right darling?* She smiles, and touches my face; being cherished and known flows from her fingers, through my skin, into places inside me that don't have names.

We sit face-to-face, she with a loaded syringe and the soft cotton thong we use as a tourniquet. *Don't go away,* she whispers going to the other side of the room to reset Annie. Dropping down again, so close. I pump up my arm and tap up a vein.
Shall I put my fingers inside you?
Just breathe with me please.

She falls into my eyes.

I push the needle in, jack it back, thrilled as always by my red, red blood. I release the thong and push in the plunge, play with it a little like I do, jack it in and out, orchestrating the rush. Annie Lennox sings, *Love is the Drug*, and Sam is right here watching me come.

More kissing and licking. I'm teasing Sam, diverting her from her turn with the gun. I know what I'm doing, pushing her, making her hot. I know where she cracks, and she does. We play such dangerous games.

She's begging me now. *Put it in Lani. Please baby*. It's the same voice she uses when she needs me to fuck her. This woman, she tears me apart. I take her arm and wrap it, tap it; put the needle straight into her big vein. I could do this to Sam in the dark. I push it in fast, the way she likes it best, and see her whole aura change colour. Watching her rush.

We are laughing now, heading for our big bed. Falling on it, into, over, twisting and slip-sliding our bodies in this holy communion that knows the way like rivers do. This morning it is long, soft, stripped-to-the-bone-of-vulnerability sex that we need. We go so deep there is nowhere left to hide anything. We orgasm at the same time, shouting and weeping in libidinal joy and gratitude. Coming in utter sync is a blessing from heaven, and when we are so blessed we always shout and weep.

We have gone down into the underworld together and know the places we are broken, where shame had been a military dictatorship. We trace each other's battle scars, and love the most unlovable in ourselves and each other.

My hand rests on her chest, her precious heart pumps beneath her skin.
I love you.
I know, she whispers, before dropping like she does in these moments, into sleep.

I pull up the sheet, walk to the window and pull sand-coloured velvet drapes across the bright Sydney morning. I light a candle, and climb back in beside my love, fold my body around her, resting my head. I wonder if she might wake me up later with sex. I like to wake up and find her fucking me.

I am home.

The story above became a play.
I don't remember exactly when I wrote it. In 1999, my friend Zoe

Reason, then working in theatre production and now a yoga teacher, was commissioned to create and direct a collection of five fifteen-minute plays by women writers. They would rotate as the opening act for Germaine Greer's adaptation of Lysistrara: The Sex Strike, *being produced by the Battersea Arts Centre. The original is dated 411BC. Greer's adaptation received mixed reviews.*

I reworked it into a play, giving Lani two voices (two actors).

The set was spare.
It worked.

It is a retrospective expression of my longing. It is my particular version of a romance, infused with the magical thinking and delusion of the Romantic Love narrative.

The real story, the one that happened, is alluded to in this fiction. It is there as a thread of what didn't triumph. It did though, and when I was hanging by the thinnest thread off the edge of this world, I did choose life. It did not however roll like this, and I reckon writing this romance was a little gift to the one that stayed, and crawled, stumbled, fell, bled, and kept going anyway. It's an exquisite chocolate on the pillow of an unfathomably expensive bespoke hotel suite. I would actually relish that hotel, and the chocolate, same as I kind of love this fairy story. My heart is there, foolish, human and recognizable as mine.

It's only subversive at all because my longing for the holy communion, the union of perfect attunment, is set in a most unlikely storyline. It is, though, the same storyline that takes early traumatic absence hostage, and tells us that romantic love will make us whole. Thing is we are already whole, and broken, and nothing is a problem to be solved.

Nevertheless, I can quote my own last line of this little romance, and trust truth. I am home, and home doesn't go anywhere, even when I get lost and parts of me forget.

Me

If I could start over.

Not necessarily my whole life (I wouldn't trust another childhood) but a clean page. Sunday afternoon with this cluster of women writing together. If I could only wind it back and find a place to start over.

I long for a place where words fall out like they mean it. All these words happening inside, making rhyme and reason of some kind; singing my song. Not these little cars that drive full force into wall after wall.

If I could start over,
I'd cherish being young,
be much kinder to the little lost soul that only knew how to cultivate hate and pain.

If I could start over, I'd tell her much sooner than so much later, that she's a honey and a dear.

Me 2

I want to go home.
What do you mean? Asked the head doctor.

I wake up in the night. It's hazy dark, not black dark. I'm looking for something, and when I unfold my body from the bed, I find pebbles in my mouth.

I'm asleep and I'm looking for you.

I am hungry and scared.
When I touch myself, my body disappears.

I am asleep, and my body has melted, and I have to find something called you.
I'm running without any feet, and screaming, though no sound can be heard.

I am asleep, and looking everywhere for you.
I am hungry and horrible.

When I reach out to touch, my body disappears.
I am asleep and my body is gone, and I have to find something called you.
I am running without any feet. I cannot find anything. Anywhere.

I am asleep, and it's horrible. I am looking everywhere without any eyes, and running without any feet. My mouth is full of pebbles.

Something like poems

Found a List

Cushion
Orange
Feathers
Rest
Sink
Support
Fabric
John Lewis
Silk
Velvet
Teacher
Foam
Tender
Woolworths
Habitat
Sensual
Georgie
Indian
Cat
Sofa
Pile
Cave
Folds

Touch
Blind
Tantra
Smell
Burrow
History
JAN
Pillows
Lean
Making Love
Weaving
Prop
Contain
Window
Myrtle
Longing
Drown
Garden
Oils
Knees
Back
Table
Layers
Sweaty
Intimate
Kavitaa
Loss
Stains
Mum
Dog Bed
Headache
Death

Abundance
Hippy
Group
Circles

Love & Gratitude

Woke up, buried under sand bags and bricks
Was rescued by Leonard The Dog.
He finds me under the rubble, every morning
Employing various techniques of retrieval.

Dog kisses
The Bark of Longing
Throwing his bed up in the air
Hunting down the sheepskin rug.

Finally, he pulls my bedding off
And I give up, give in, give myself over
To serving my dog.

It makes me laugh
How he gets me moving
Like no amount of therapy, or prayers
Or any manner of good intentions
and useless will.

Today, we walked in the colours of autumn
He fell in love with the most enormous Deerhound
And lost himself completely in the joy of it.
He shows me stuff like this, every day.
Thank you, Leonard The Dog.

Please

I have lost a few pieces of myself
along the road
it always felt like dying
until I made a friend of death
now I live on my knees
and whisper prayers
oh, please take me
take another piece of me

Rest

the day after I drowned
i woke on the seabed
i could breathe

high up above
through the water shadows and light
i could hear that other world

some people were looking for me
i tried to send a message up
I'm okay all is well
I don't think they could hear it

Sleep

she wakes up late
in a hot damp bed
in a room full of light
reaching through the borders
of another brand-new day

she pants and wheezes
like a sick old dog
and her morning mouth
tastes of despair
she's lost the plot not
the plot exactly
but her hard won
soft strong faith
that life is mad and beautiful
and always everything at once
and that all is well
even when it isn't

she doesn't believe that anymore
and wants to go on home
everywhere she looks
she sees her stories
scattered like shipwrecks
on the rocks

she wants to lie down on moss
in the roots of a big old tree
underneath leaves
and oh, so quietly
run out of breath

Candles

I keep a candle burning in the bedroom
and you may not be surprised to hear
in the kitchen.

On Sundays, I light a long-tapered candle
often, but not always blue
I say, thank you life
for another week.

Having just performed this small ritual
I notice my gratitude is not convinced.

I used to think Grace had a certain aesthetic
now I know that Grace is Grace.
That light doesn't mind
if I swear and bleed
the candles forgive me every time.

Day List

- Bought cat food
- Welcomed three men (two dressed – one not)
- Amended list
- Crossed fingers
- Got lily pollen on my face from breathing in those sexy things

Throat Song

A song lives in Leonard.
It is most particular,
not from his belly nor lungs,
yet informed by breath.

The sound tenderness makes
love distilled to spirit.
Sometimes, I imagine this world
without Leonard in it.

Terror and heart merge,
fell me to my knees.
I stay down there
until I can open again.

Sometimes when I lay on the Table of Mercy
in the skilful hands of my osteopath,
the same noise happens in my throat.
I am reminded of how he lives in me

in my blood and bones
and in my very own throat song.
I do wonder if somewhere, just out of sight,
he might be writing a poem about me.

Empty

In the cup of my hands
I find empty
It looks like Antarctica
It looks like my kind
of empty

Funny how much energy
It has taken
to keep it at bay
and now
I am kind of in love
with all the shades and tones
of white on white
on white

the distance between
being in
and coming out
is a hard road
to a sometimes
but not always
soft place

the distance between
finger and hip
a window and a wall
between the window ledge
and the fall
between this breath
and the next
between this breath
and death
the distance between
flesh and bone
home and away
coming and going

In the cup of my hands
I find it all
and lose it again

my own dear body
is a ravaged prayer
or should that be
ravaged body
tender prayer

I live here
between heaven and earth
tethered to both
and to neither
it has taken a long time
to recognise my own smell
and taste

It takes me
a long time
to get anywhere
or nowhere
a long time to arrive
on any kind of dance floor
in any kind of rhythm

I live between heaven and earth
In a body I am not sure I recognise
despite our long years together –
tongue searches my mouth
for a taste
of something like home
like touching the nerve
in an exposed tooth

I didn't even realise
I had it all the time
I had it in my belly
and in my homeless heart

I think we are all praying
if we know it or not
It's just what I think
not in any hard-line way

I mean, I won't knock at your door
and ram my prayer
down your throat

I am here

for Colin Harrison

I am here –
It has taken a long time to be able to say that
with truth and conviction,
with simple –

I am here in the world.

I got lost, tangled, and trapped in the tangled
my weary head explodes with ideas
about what should and shouldn't be.

I didn't know, until I did, that I have always been here.
Waiting. Lonely. Uncertain. Longing.

Of course, it is never one Hollywood Homecoming,
but a series of small recognitions, whispered welcomes,
tiny out-breaths of relief.

I keep coming home, and sometimes my knees bleed.
My heart kisses those knees.

I am not only in the world
I am the world
I am kinship
I am every speck of everything
I am the killer and the killed
I am the helpless and the dictator
I am the brightest light
I am the darkest night.

I am screaming, pleading, begging for mercy,
I am deaf to it all.

I am *fuck you, fuck off, fuck everything*,
kill everything, give up on everything.
I am hate: murderous, weapons of mass destruction hate,
stamp on, stamp-it-all to extinction hate.
I am the child that wanted to die
and wanted to kill, from that terrible place.

What if all the killers were once that child,
and we grow from that ground,
the ground below that,
and build systems, armies, ideas
that separate each one of us, from ourselves
and each-other.

And this precious, ravaged land is dying
because we just don't know any more
how not to be killers
how not to be separate.

I am here
I am in the world
I am home.

The *'welcome to it all'* mat is on the doorstep,
and sometimes I forget all of the above,
safe finally in the knowledge that I will
remember again.

Walls & Rooms

I have itchy writing fingers
there's something to say
I know not what.
There's a whole orchestra of mystery
more chaos than harmonious
instruments all crying out at once.
In the orchestra pit
under my ribs sometimes the chaos
Is okay. Sometimes not at all okay.

Today it is noise, energy, itchy fingers
and questions with no form
and no answers.

It has been making me think about walls
and how fragile they are
how easily they are destroyed
by bombs, floods and fire.

If we're lucky, we're here
within the walls of our houses and flats
inside our rooms, or our huts or tents
or nowhere with walls at all.

This government is filling empty hotel rooms
with homeless people
not to help them but to help contain COVID-19

Kisses

kiss everything
the bloody and the maimed

kiss the back of a friend's neck
when they don't expect it

kisses are wise
they know what needs kissing

Falling

She was pushed out
of a broken mother.
A Kleinian child
without a container.

A mindless soul
in free fall
all of her life
holding the fall at bay.
Held together
by sheer will
the colours, the flashes of light
the slipping of skin.

How to fall
not fall to pieces.

Falling through time
burning stories into the flesh
sucking, biting, tearing
at the breast of death.

Swallowing, injecting, pushing into
every last crevice of herself
hate, violation, madness and pain.

Always falling
but not calling
catch me.

Tears

tropical rain
pours down bedroom window pane

the leaves and the vines
like jungle

the sky is crying
I haven't poured for years

the last time I did I never wanted to stop
it was heaven on a blue dance floor

Parts

This car is me
all the parts
the totality of Caro.

I have a home address
a welcome mat
a blue front door.

Maybe the car drove me home
maybe the car and the house
are the same place.

Sometimes the car has to pull off the road
park up overlooking an ocean until breathing
and settling happens.

The car has taught me
still does
that it's all about who drives.

Tiny baby newborn parts impotent rage
helpless hopeless parts
the I can't go on I give up leave me alone.

To bow to each and every speck
of how they came to help
to protect to help me survive to make it to the place.

We can't bring home the homeless
without help and helping
the grace of the places where welcome to everything

is the ground, the culture, the village
the places where staying with what was so lonely
and trapped in concrete separated parts

so loud and unforgiving are all just ushered in
be as you are
you are already here.

Already all right already precious always enough
here are the mirrors here are the invitations here is the
   place
the most hurt and far away parts
have been waiting and waiting
and hoping
and not daring to hope

would one day open a doorway even a crack
and a part you maybe don't even know is there
hears a whisper of welcome

and maybe the beginning of knowing: I am not alone
the tiniest seed of that
falls into a soil.

Even if our parts are kicking up a storm of protest
no this is not for me they are weird, losers I don't belong,
bla bla bla.

Nevertheless some tiny seeds fell into some earth
some of them help me in different ways
some of them just need reassurance that I'm still here.

Some of them get activated at very inconvenient moments
I wake up every morning in my *NO TO EVERYTHING*
I have found a way to greet her meet her be patient with
  her (mostly).

I just know it is me holding me
that thing that Christians say: *God doesn't go anywhere*
but we can drift away.

It's like that
even in the wildest tsunami (I was in one recently)
home didn't go anywhere.

That's not nothing
I'm blessed to know the tragicomedy of our precious little
  lives
tender and absurd

we struggle and tangle and suffer and believe we are a
  problem
needing to be solved
a bit like not remembering where the car came from

I don't know when my heart
found this frequency or when enough fell away for me to
  meet tenderness comedy
I'm just grateful.

All my parts were taken hostage by shame
now they trust me
and they trust you
the ones that have walked alongside me

as I have you
they trust you to say things
that would have been impossible to hear.

As clean clear water
not the other
the old stuff

the hard-earned freedom to hear a callout
what are you doing caro
and know including an ouch

that it's just love trust and safe happening
yep
that's me and my parts.

Day

I wake up – I groan
I say, okay day

I smooth the cat
& drink diet coke in bed

I bake a cake
I please a man

I bake another cake
I dance

I prance
I sing along with Leonard

I say thank you, out loud, a lot
I kiss the cat

Same Old Shit

Don't breathe deep
Don't say a word, especially any true ones
Especially not with feeling

Don't make a fuss
Don't make a sound
Don't need anything

No mess
Be quiet
Disappear

Don't have a body
or a hunger
or genitals

or a bottom that poos
Don't smile at yourself
or meet a stranger's eye

Don't hope
Don't dream of being you
because you don't fucking exist

Don't ask for help
or offer it (who do you think you are?)
Don't make plans

or imagine it might ever be different
What I don't say is
I need you whoever you are

I don't say – *Help me I'm scared*
I don't say – *Please listen to me no not just the juice. A lot
Please help me ride this wave.*

No I don't say that
I don't won't can't say – *I can't go on*
I don't say – *Please find me where I've hidden*

I find you instead
I don't scream or whisper
I tell you who I am.

Kissing Bears

I kissed a bear today
in the woods
in the Circle of Life.

We – the bear and me
we held the feet
of a wounded child

inside a healing man
in the Circle of Life.
I lunched with a bear

and many other animals
I returned to the woods
I buried a golden ring

my mother wore for 40 years
on her finger
I held it first in my soft closed fist

until it fell into the kind earth
beneath a very old tree
yesterday that tree had my back

as I vomited truth and bile
out of the earth inside me

I was seen
I was held
I was safe

I kissed a bear today
in the woods
in the Circle of Life.

You Again

it's you again this morning
can't i meet another face
can't i score a bit of grace

it makes me tired
this waking up
and waking up again
a day is like an empty road
a desert sky
a ball of shame

and even though it's kind
i'm kind
i've found the land of kind
the desperate
is so desperate
and i'm lost
and lost again

it's quieter than it ever was
i can hear some prayers
that might be mine
i can hear the time move through me
and myself move through the time

i used to long for many things
now i long for less
i long to put my head down
to rest
to rest
to rest

i'm looking for a weathered rock
a salty shore
a place to put my head down
to ask for nothing more

Fran

dear fran
i do think about you
yes I do

often this happens in the kitchen
i find myself in small conversations
exchanges engages

with a woman called Fran
that is partly you
but mostly
my idea of you

Shoe List

Small shoes
School shoes
Shame shoes
Riding shoes
Plimsoles
Platform shoes
Tennis shoes
Flip flops
Stilettoes
Caterpillar boots
Doc Martens
Sea shoes
Dance shoes
Birkenstocks
Crocs
No shoes

Key

Depression
Relentless
Even in the fields of kindness
Relentless

I don't know how I managed
for so long
for so long

before I realised
I had the key
to the fields of kindness
hidden

in my own
hand

Circles

I have come to rely
on what we make together
I feel safe in our place

The outpost where we pitch a tent
push and pull some big rocks
into a ragged circle

I have come to rely on
the moving constellations of matter
as we follow our own footsteps

back and forward to basecamp
each time with hands so empty
and so full

Being Seen

If I hadn't fashioned these words
into this vague cluster and shape
you would never ever know
how death defying it was
to get here and speak them.

I employed a combination of compassion
and brute force
with strategies of commitment and service
to get my landlocked sandbagged body
to the kitchen.

Somehow out of this particular forcefield
came the lightest of all lyrical cakes.
You might not imagine I live like this
or even think of me at all
if I didn't pin down and capture

these fragments of death defiance
the effort of getting through each day.
My defeat would never see the light
if I didn't show you
the only way I know how.

Despair

If I were a better poet
I could make a better poem
out of repetition and defeat.

I am bent over another desperate day
a ramshackle sack of broken tools and rust
dragging along behind.

I even miss violence from the past
the years before I found the Fields of Kindness
and forgave myself for being depressed.

On certain days I do miss destruction
That freedom to rip myself to pieces
Flying broken and bloody into the winds.

Birthday

another thin blue candle
to say thank you life
for another week
and on this occasion
another year

how sweet to meet
my gratitude
dancing quietly
with my longing
to retreat

i think it was me that said
all one damned and beautiful river
i have reached
the beginning of being old
am astonished

and touched
to find so much simplicity
waiting patiently for me to arrive

1460 Days with Leonard

Oh my, I am depressed
you might well say
what's new
I might well say that too.

I've supersized up, I've got
depressed with extra fries
I'm looking for a love song
for Leonard.

Depressed has got my tongue
my eyelids can't go on
I am on a respirator
though you might not see that

at first glance.
Just a crooked woman
with a beautiful dog
searching her muffled heart
for a way to thank him.

A Prayer

oh don't go – don't leave me in the world
what matters
tell me that then
if you can tell me what matters

terrible noises struggle out of my mouth
into this placeless place
please watch me from the gate in the field
now darling it's my turn to fall

muffled words disappear
as I try and kiss your face
will you cradle me, lay down
with me, write something on my body

with yours
breath through trees
my ravaged heart my fingers and tongue
humans on our knees

A Life in a Day

knitting and weeping
birthday cake and two clients
a day in the life

rose flew in and out
pyjamas on and dinner
a day in the life

the west wing again
leonard kisses closed eyelids
a day in the life

another pee walk
nod to neighbours and the moon
a day in the life

candle light and a pill
dog snuffles
another day done

Questions

Do I need to get up
stand up, do this
show and tell myself
to you?

Do I need to riff and roll
whisper, and/or shout?
Do I need to
keep doing this?

Speak to you, myself and God
like this?
Little mind has judgements
mindless mind pays no mind

Trust happens somewhere
that doing THIS
offer up my mumbled prayers
secrets longings my defeat

is how I make love
how I stay here
I touch you
I receive your touch

all over my shattered battered
skin and bones
into all the holes cracks and crevices
I let you in like this

inside all the no-go hatches
the places no one no not ever
said welcome called me sweetheart
or squeezed my hand

such a long walk, walking, from there
to here –
the here that has been waiting for me
all this time

here I am like this
repeating heart beating
welcome
welcome
I am HERE
Like THIS
this thing I do
with words not quite poems

not not poems either
this thing I am doing right now
offering myself up like a song
or a cake

it works for me
a pathway not on a map
a pathway that asks me crawl blindfold
to keep finding losing and finding

my place in this world
I do need to stand up
in it looking around
saying hey

here I am with you
when I'm dead and gone
when you find
I did not write as much

as you may have expected to find
maybe you have heard my poems fall
like leaves, hard or soft rain
via email, blog world, Facebook, et al

in bedrooms bars, hospital corridors
and in all manner of circles of love

Repetition

The same old bed
where every morning
is a fall from the grace
of narcotic dreaming.

Crash land
what is
this is
here is.

I grab the soft white flesh
of my inner arm pinch it
hard.
Sound escapes my lungs

retrieving a trace memory
a thread of recall
it is always and forever new.
every bloody morning

even though
even though
it always throws me at the wall
I have grown accustomed

and my knees are calloused now
from crawling and praying my way
into each day.

Thank you teachers
for teaching me that.
You know who you are.

I remember that broken girl
the almost didn't make it girl
the girl that fell into the kindness

of lesbians the ravaged tenderness
of Leonard's songs
a few fragments of mystery
she hitches a ride into her future.

Here I stand
that girl
weathered now on the cusp of old
greedy for an early ticket out of here.

Nothing much has changed.
Look
you still go to bed a lot
and lust after death.

The distance between BedWorld now
and BedWorld then
is an epic trek of repetition and bloody knees
I can't go on.

I have left a few piles of rags
on the highways
things I thought were solid as rock,
then fell away.

The weight
of my old friend depression
has space
where there was only noise.

1992

I build a house of stone
to house my stony heart.

For decades
it has been a fortress

a homeless house
a house of cards.

Lately it has been trying
to tell me something

I need to understand.
I try too hard

my head hurts
it is a house of confused.

Which feels like failing
which is familiar and tired.

I am furious and bored
I dream of having courage enough

to pour petrol through the letter box
and set my house on fire.

Oh yes I can feel that –
violent longing to burn to become ash.

Freedom

I'm so tired.
I'm too tired.

I'm lost and found.
I'm lost & unable to go back to sleep.

I want to doze my way back
to the house of drama noise and defence
(not always, or even that often).

When I feel a sharp spike of alone
I look around see what I see
hear the one that cries.

Digging

I am digging in the darkness
in the silence
to get free
digging deep
into kind earth
a truffle pig
hunting down the hidden place
where a tiny girl buried everything
to survive
finding my way
to the source of the big secret
only this time
I am armed and dangerous
on a mission to rescue
a howling loveless child
waiting thirty years
never quite giving up hope

**Postcards to others –
some sent – some not**

Heart Daughter

Hey,
here I am again.

I bought the 1975's album, and Bakar single. I love the video of Bakar, and the song. He's luminous, and his beauty is deeply inside him. I mean of course he is a good-looking human, but being *that* doesn't make us shine. That's the inside, and is why people who are not *beautiful* in the formulaic way, just are if they are alive and burning bright from inside.

I'm sorry you and your Mom (it tickles me that Clare is Mom, not Mum. I like it) are having, or have been and are coming through a tough time. Relationship, love attachment is hardcore. It asks more of us and gives us the most, more than pretty much anything in this weird, wonderful, and unbearable thing called having a little life to live.

You are right in the eye of the storm of navigating your transition into young adulthood and it is full of tripwires and landmines.

All welcome. All part of the dance -– just keep rolling and trusting. You are both finding your way.

Clare once told me that when she asked if you knew you were loved, you said: *I've always known that.*

It made me cry.
Because I was part of your beginning.
We created an unequivocal welcome, your Mom and me.

We tuned into your frequency so we could hear you.
You were our Radio Station.
We listened to and stayed with you, and made sure you received, internalised, and were on the ground beneath your feet.

Your Mom kept on loving you like that – your ground got more solid.
Whatever you create and make of being you, is built on that ground.

Do you know you're loved?
I've always known that.

Barry

Oh Barry,
It's a funny thing, writing to the dead.
I don't know much,
but I'm pretty sure you are no longer receiving mail.

I am writing to honour and salute you.

I really hope you knew how much you mattered
to us – to many 'Ashies',
the us that lived alongside, above you, across
the road.

My battered old heart aches with the longing that you may not
have known that your kindness, your terrible jokes, your openness
to fellow human beings' attitude,
your being YOU – was precious and felt and valued,
and that you were loved,
though we don't rock and roll
around this weird business of life
saying: *Barry, mate, we love you.*

Maybe we should do that more?
I think we should,
given how fragile our little lives are,
how we mostly never know
when we are going to go.

I would think that,
being a 5-star old hippy.
You mattered to me
and to Leonard The Dog,
who for a while thought all men in crash helmets
were you. We let you call him Lenny,
only you though,
we made an exception, because it was you.

I hadn't signed my non-Christmas card
before you slipped from this life, into being gone
whatever that means.
I don't know much,
but I know you are free.
It is us that look into that space
where you no longer are –
we will keep on missing you there.

Birthday Poem for Sue

I've been hunting down a poem
a special one, for you.
I've been calling for the words
to unfurl, to drift in on the wing
like birds coming home.

I've tried too hard
to make a pitch perfect poem
a happy birthday poem.

Orgasmic sex,
tears and poems get further away
the harder we chase them.

I only wanted to say
that I treasure and cherish
and love you.

Sometimes, I am embarrassed
by just how much I do.
I get over it though
and keep saying thank you.

I will be saying: *Thank you, Sue*
for the rest of my life
and this clumsy collection of words
is only a verse in that song.

Dear Nick

these helpless words
are my hunger
to touch see feel you
to attend that wonderful friends & dinner
you wanted to make
before your hunger disappeared

your hunger disappeared
and then you died

I thought I would have
a long time to be your friend

Love Letter to Jan

I like to walk. To be clear about this, when I say *walk,* I don't mean trek, or hike, or marathon walk.

I do not even own walking boots, though I wouldn't mind a pair to be honest.

I like to walk gently, slowly, as an alternative to getting on a tube or a bus.

I like to walk from my front door in Queen's Park to Finchley Road Waitrose, or in the other direction to Notting Hill. I like to walk and breathe, walk and think, or especially walk and not think. Sometimes I write poems when I walk, and then they disappear. I feel sad when that happens.

This is a very short story about a particular walk.

The relentless treading of a circular path, or you could say backwards and forwards. It is a walk with a short train ride sandwiched in between the walking. Overground Line, Brondesbury Park to Hampstead Heath Station.

My bedroom or kitchen, to your hospital bed in the Royal Free Hospital.

Over and over and over again, and now this walk is over. It's done.

To be honest, I don't miss that walking.

I miss you.

Song for the Motherless

what if you never had a true taste of holding
what if you never knew it
it was never yours
never imprinted on your tiny helpless being
what if you never knew the deep relaxation of being held
being precious
being welcome
being enough

these things we don't carry in our mind
in this language in this kind of remembering
in the baby bones of us

what if you never knew this blessing
gift birthright
what if you never knew the homeland
of deep peace and surrender
the bedrock of holding
the nowhere to go here already
just this moment
just this

what if you carry the agony
of the fiercest hungers and the defeat
and they are driving your wild and precious life
down the train tracks
of pain and repetition
and what if this is not the only thing that can happen
even though it was
the only thing that could happen

what if there is a holy mother of love and mercy
with her arms open wide as barn doors
saying *I am here I am right here*
Lean in. Put your head down. I have got you.
Breathe out. And in again. And out.

what if this mother is you
always has been
always has been here
in your own field of kindness
in the chamber of your own precious heart

we don't know how to hold what needs holding
if we inherited absence
if we were dropped by the wounding
of our own mothers
and their mothers
and so on down the line

sometimes it takes a few generations
and a lot of blood on those tracks (forgive me Mr. Dylan)
to get home
to the heartbroken simplicity
of holding the baby
that wasn't held

Client

You slipped in through one of Leonard's cracks,
those cracks where light comes in.

You needed me,
I was right there,
You needed me.

We began to walk you Home,
I was the mother, the mirror,
the one that saw and felt you,
that recognised
how deeply lonely, desperate even
for the one already here, you were.

Waiting, longing, not knowing
if you would ever turn round
and see way,
way back behind you,
lost and trapped inside old stories
that never made any sense
because they just weren't true.

Those stories got inside,
into bone, muscle, blood
and into vital organs: heart,
lungs, pancreas, spleen
carrying a poison that was never yours
into miles of gut and stomach.

Somehow you let me take your tiny bird-bone shoulders,
and I, without really knowing either, trusted
you needed me to help you turn around,
to follow the breadcrumb trail backwards,
where you were bound up tight in ropes,
woven out of legacy, lineage, history repeating
the story of you
that wasn't you
wasn't ever you.

You felt me feeling you
and trusted leaning into
what every single human being needs.
To be felt, listened to through our first and only language
that is embodied and helpless.

Otherwise, we land in absence, empty space, and we fall.
Unsafe and alone become the foundation stone on which we write
ourselves.

Even though there is noise, and people
to feed and water you, give you shelter from the storm
there is no one there to feel and hear you,
so you are truly alone.

For a long time, although we spoke of many things,
many things that mattered, what mattered most
was you leaning into being felt and stayed with.

The thing about this – is the staying, is the happening,
Is the unspoken tuning in, the holding of an inconsolable baby
while we feel into themes, and patterns and storylines. All the places
your precious life had fallen down holes
over and over, different holes, same story.

All those hours, over years,
the staying with, the fighting with, the grief,
the times you needed to hate me and have me stay anyway.
All those years and hours and staying,
my staying,
your staying,
the staying with becoming yours,
the safe harbour is inside you.

You are your own home address,
there is a place now, a cradle woven out,
all those hours of staying and being stayed with.

And if there is a kind of mothering in this,
it is not quite the same as Mother and Baby.
The Original.

This is something else, medicinal, over-pathologised in some schools of thought in other places, something else.

Here, this is a story that I took very seriously, because we should never, ever offer holding, if we don't have enough ourselves.

However under construction our own cradle is,
to know that being a cradle, a place, a space, an invitation to lean in, is always however flawed, imperfect, full of cracks – about commitment, and capacity to be in service to the other.

Enough – to know it in your bones and blood, enough, as Mr. Winnicott would say
good enough, to know that it is not for you.

It will give you more than you can grasp, but only as it asks for stretching into mystery, carnage, being lost and found, going mad, being mad without being toxic – clean mad tastes different, and it is sometimes, not always, where this thing called psychotherapy is a holy healing mess.

I find a pathway though writing – it shows me what I didn't know, and
knowing less and trusting more is the cradle my baby keeps on falling
into.

The here that has no name, no address, no promised land, but just is here, and that in the beginning it was always me in imperfect remembering, this is for you, and that helped me help you – and now we are free.

Both free.
Both broken and whole.

Both mother and child, not just for the you and the me, but for something more – for the un-nameable, the borderless, the hopeless and impossible business of being so human, compelled to love and to need, and make new humans and love them without understanding anything at all.

Going to Ireland

Sometimes I fall through the noise
and land in something like Grace
or a Field of Kindness
or a Sea of Simplicity.

It doesn't really matter what it's called,
I know it,
it is empty, and full.
I know nothing, except for what matters
and that would slip through the eye of a needle.

I know all I have to give
is little me, my little life.

I remember standing in Tuscan woods with Massimo
a long time ago,
he said, *Caroline, you are the light. It lives in you*
he said, *You are full of longing – give yourself up to it*
he saw me like a father would see a daughter
he said, *Caroline, I see you.*

it was a moment.

Massimo died on Christmas day,
I think in 2017, but it could have been 2018,
my heart breaks for Susie who loved him,
slept and woke with him.
Matteo, his beautiful son,
his granddaughter,
the people who had him in their daily lives,
and have to live with the space where he isn't.

Me, I know that he flew out of his mortal body like a firefly.

We give ourselves to each other,
this little group, that in my mind
I call, going to Ireland.

This place where each of us is the gift of our own precious beam of light,
there is no manual for being that,
we are as we are.
Lost, found, silent, hidden, noisy, angry, broken, holy, always holy (as Patti Smith would say),

in this place, everything that matters, is tiny
and huge
and slips through the eye of a needle
and, as Leonard once sang,

And the blessings come from heaven
And for something like a second
I'm cured and my heart
Is at ease.

thank you, as ever, which as ever feels inadequate
though it is all I've got
everything I've got.

I love you, caro xx

Stroking naked men

Stroking Naked Men

I started stroking naked men for money in 2007. It feels light years ago. Not so much in linear distance, but more in the sense of understanding from this later perspective what it was I was doing.

It shook me with its clarity, simplicity and insistence.
My mind had a lot to say about how I couldn't and shouldn't, not least about the potential pitfalls in my being a long-time practising psychotherapist.

When the mind-noise abated enough it became simple. I had to step forward. With rigorous consideration, thought, consultation with trusted others, but mostly with the core part of me to whom it only made sense.

I set it up, with the baseline condition being if it felt wrong (for me) in any way, even if I didn't exactly know why, I would trust that feeling and step back out again.

It proved to be a doorway to so much.
I didn't know, but I did trust.

I purchased a second phone and distilled an invitation into a twenty-word classified. I hung out my shingle and started work.

This is what I knew. I wanted to create and offer intimacy within a structure. To use what I'd learned over two decades as a therapist, about how to hold space and attention. I wanted to touch rather than handle people, and lovingly offer pleasure rather than mechanistically get them off.

Men started rolling in. I learned how to use the telephone as a portal and to pick up the attitude underneath the words. I said 'No' a lot. I was weeding out anger and contempt, and the colour palate of misogyny. I could hear it crouched and hiding in the most charming and articulate, as palpably as its more obvious counterpart.

This is how it goes with my naked men: a phone call leading to an appointment. Leading to a man on my doorstep at a designated time. Leading to him being invited in, welcomed and settled. I take a little time to say hello, and to let him take me in. I check if there's anything he'd like to ask or say before I get him unwrapped and up on the table. Over and over again, over these years, I've stood in this beginning moment with many men. It always pulses with vulnerability. Always. And I've come to appreciate the beauty of this very particular vulnerability. It takes courage for men to walk into erotic tenderness; a different kind of courage than that required for combat.

I now deeply understand what the chapter I call Stroking Naked Men, both asked of and gave to me.

I was going to make a memoir called just that.

I didn't write it though, and these are a few tiny threads of what didn't become a book that I think would have touched some in the reading, in much the way the work itself touched each naked recipient, and myself in the devotion of my practice.

It gave me myself in the field of libidinal joy.

I learned that *holding the frame* is my favourite sexual position, perhaps the only one I can truly occupy in freedom. I was in my glory days, and gratitude doesn't even touch the sides of what it means to have been so healed.

I've had more sex than many humans, most of it informed by the formative experience from very early, un-remembered years.

I'm sad I haven't made 'Stroking Naked Men' (& the occasional woman) as a whole book. A sex and money memoir from a different country than the one they are usually written from.

Here sit a few tiny fragments from the abandoned construction site of an unwritten memoir.

A Phone Call

Hello.

Is that Carolina?

Yes it is.

I saw your advert in the paper. Can I come and see you today?

Maybe, I say. *I can do a massage today as it happens. Later on. Let's back up a bit first though. Tell me something about what you're looking for.*

Oh, you know, just a massage with a happy ending.

I smile at him. *I would describe my service as a devoted pleasuring throughout, rather than a rub-down and a wank.*

Okay, he says. *That's fine.*

Would you like to ask me any more questions?

No, no, it's fine. Can I come this afternoon? I finish work at four.

I could offer you an appointment around four. I listen carefully to this man that isn't saying much. I prod him a little. *Are you sure?*

You can have a think if you like and call me back.

No, he says. *I want to come. I will show up.*

Right you are, I say. I decide he's one of mine. I can sniff something underneath his monosyllabic efforts that feels true. *Okay, so let me tell you what I charge.*

Okay, he says.

I tell him my fee.

That's fine, he says.

Good, I say, getting into his rhythm. *You'd better tell me your name.*

It's Clive.

I imagine shaking hands with him. I give him the address and information about parking. *Looking forward to finding you on my doorstep in a couple of hours,* I say.

Okay. Bye.

Bye, Clive.

I plant a small kiss on my phone and write him into my day.

Another Phone Call

Hello. A tiny beat of anxious comes down the line before I hear his voice.

Hello, he says. *Is that Carolina?*

Yes it is.

Ah. Well. I saw your ad in the newspaper, and I wonder ... He stumbles and coughs. *I wonder if you could give me some information.*

I can, I say, and sit down in my kitchen. I'm covered in flour and sugar and the air smells like an idea of childhood. I start to answer this question I've been asked so many times over the past five years, by so many men.

My spiel goes something like this.

I offer a beautiful bespoke erotic massage, I tell him. *It's an intimate and sensual treat from the moment I open the door to you until I show you out again. I am not a massage parlour, and it is not a conveyer belt of men. I have other work that I love, and do all that I do because it matters to me and I do it well.* I pause. *I would say I'm most compatible with those that seek a pleasurable encounter offered with warmth and connection. Those who would like to be touched rather than handled.*

Oh, he says. *That sounds very nice. You sound nice.*

Thank you. I am nice. I smile into the phone.

I've been for a few massages at different places. I know I want something, and it goes okay, but I usually end up feeling crap and wishing I hadn't bothered.

I'm guessing you get a rub down and a wank from someone who isn't very interested in what she's doing.

He laughs. *That's it exactly*, he says. *I feel empty after.*

Lonely? I ask.

Yes, bloody lonely. Stupid to do it really. But you sound different from that.

Yes I am, I agree. *Other end of the spectrum, the human end. Now, what's your name?*

David.

Hello David, I say. I hear him breathe out and then in again. I go on. *I believe that some of the men that use sexual services are looking for intimacy and contact. Intimacy is a word many of us use instead of sex. Sex isn't intimacy, though it can be found there, and most sexual services are delivered in a mechanistic way. If you are on the receiving end of an erotic massage given by somebody that is going through the motions and isn't really there in contact, however skilful they are, you will feel the absence, feel it as lonely.*

Yes, he says simply.

I do the opposite. I give you a real welcome with my real self, which you feel of course, so you know I'm really with you. And, because it makes my heart happy to do this work and give like this, you feel that too.

You sound very genuine, he says.

My unique selling point, I smile at him from my kitchen and wonder where he is. *I show up. I create that atmosphere by doing so and welcome you into it. It makes me sound like a bit of an old hippie, which is indeed a thread of my heritage, it is an honour to do this.* I pause. *For me there is a direct link between sex, tenderness and vulnerability; an exquisite kind of nakedness that is not about having or not having clothes on.*

I remember out loud; *A couple of years ago, when I was interviewed for a Sunday supplement, I said, I am always aware that when I have a man's cock in my hand, I am also holding his heart.* The Sunday Times *wouldn't let me say cock though."* I laugh and so does David.

I like you.

I like you too, I say, touched as always by just how simple it can be.

So what happens now? he asks.

You may have more questions. You may want to go away and feel into what it's been like to have this conversation, and see if you'd like to book a session. You might want to make an appointment right now.

Yes please, he says. *I'd like an appointment. I absolutely want to meet you.*

I tell him about the geography and the cost, and book him in for three days time.

I'm excited, he tells me. *I wish it was today.*

Delicious anticipation, I suggest.

Bloody hell, he mutters sweetly, *me too*.

We say goodbye. I write him into my diary sheet and return to cake world.

Same world.

This Phone Call

I pick up the telephone.

It has been a million times now.

Hello.
Is that Carolina?
It is.
Okay. How much do you charge?

I tell him my fees.

And, what do I get for that?
A warm welcome and a sublime massage.
Do you do oral sex?
Sometimes I do, though not to order.

Puzzled pause (my interpretation).

You mean I wouldn't definitely get oral?
That's right.
So if you liked me, you'd suck me off?
If I felt it was part of the medicine you needed, it would happen.
Medicine?
Yes, medicine.

Pause.

Okay. I'll have to think about it and call you back.

Okay, I say, and roll on with my day.

The One That Didn't Pay

I don't remember exactly when I stopped asking my naked men to pay at the beginning of their session. It was what I used to do as routine, and now it isn't.

I didn't really notice that change happening.

Sometimes they pay upfront anyway. Both regulars and newbies do this, so I have relaxed into sometimes being paid at the beginning and sometimes at the conclusion.

Paying before is a sex industry norm and initially I just did it without thinking too hard. What I started to observe and feel was that for some it was a jarring note. A small ouch that made a tear in the delicate fabric of welcome and contact. It is, I believe, because of noticing that, that my practice has changed.

The one that didn't pay was an ordinary sort of chap. He didn't have so much to say in an ordinary, unforthcoming sort of way. He telephoned in the morning and came later that afternoon where I had a space to offer.

I sat him down in my blue room and invited him to tell me what he needed. This is often a tricky question, and I ask it more to learn who I am with. I can often hear the whispers of what isn't possible to put into words; the longings and the lonely.

I heard him okay in the muffled and mumbled. I know this code, so although it is always unique, it is familiar and I get the gist of who has come to me for something he doesn't know he needs.

I get into my rhythm and groove of unwrapping a man. What I did hear in myself but overrode was a little intuitive voice telling me to ask him to pay before we started. I nearly did, and then I missed the moment. I told myself: *it's fine*.

The massage was sexy and sweet.
I was in the swing of my dance. I found him and was allowed to touch much more humanity than his body.

After he orgasmed, he shut down in a micro second, and all that I'd been allowed to see, touch and be close to – disappeared. This does happen, and it always hurts my heart.

I get it.
I understand that being found, seen and stayed with is exposing. I let him be as he rushed back into his clothes, pushing all my usual offers of water, washing options and gentle transitional space, unequivocally away.

Once he was repackaged he went through an elaborate performance of having left his wallet at home. There was a micro heartbeat in me, wanting to believe him, but it wasn't true and we both knew that.

I looked him in the eye and his eyes rolled away.

It will catch up with you, I said as I showed him out. *You've just taken a perfectly sincere human being for a dirty ride. I hope it was worth it.*

As for me?

Well, it reminded me to listen more respectfully to what I know, to what I hear.

I wondered, fruitlessly of course, if he'd have paid if I'd asked him to prior to the unwrapping. I suspect he would. I think he took advantage of the opportunity I gave him to keep the hundred and twenty pounds in his pocket.

Naked Man

He came in from the cold.

A tall man wrapped inside good clothes, lightly dusted with snowflakes.

Sorry, he said, at the same moment I said, *Welcome*.

He couldn't keep eye contact for long. His gaze skittered and ripples of anxiety rolled off him, falling into this kindest of rooms.

I take his hand in mine, breathe for both of us, slow breathing, feeling his nervous system begin to settle.

Barely perceptible cracks appear on the surface of his skin. I am allowed to slip into him – I tell him he is safe. I land in his micro capacity for trusting that.

Almost nothing happens.

After that day, he comes to my front door approximately every six weeks. He lets me unwrap him, each time allowing the nothing happening to deepen.

One time, I take his face so gently in between my hands, and my mouth finds his mouth. The almost-nothing-that-happens in this kissing brings tears. They roll down his face into our mouths.

Snow Man

It takes a few minutes to drop down into my body, into the beating of my own heart. Into this now familiar position.

Familiar, even though it is brand new each and every time. Brand new if I am welcoming a regular, or a brand-new human.

I stand at the bottom of the table and take his feet into my hands.

The sun slithers in through the cracks of closed shutters, light dapples and dances in my blue room.

I hold his feet in my hands and breathe. He breathes. I start to find him, this long, lean, spare man, laying unwrapped on my table, while light dances over his skin.

I start to find him.

I drizzle him in warm oil, stroking gently into his skin, and his soul, what I have to offer. I feel his bones underneath and the proximity of vital organs. I feel the small pulses, tiny waves moving under my fingers. I touch a bruise inside his right thigh and wonder what made this mark on this man.

I am starting to find him.

I see a snowscape. I see a conspiracy of whites and shades of night that would break a heart or kill a soldier. I am tasting an unfathomable longing in this quiet man.

I take him in, as much as he can allow. I taste the snow in him. I taste the fire at the core of his ice. I taste his privacy and recognise it.

I take him in as much as I can bear.

I kiss the bird wing of his shoulder blade. I stand on the ground where this is what I do, with his head in my hands. I touch his face, his eyebrows, the edge of his mouth. I hold his skull in my hands.

I am astonished to be allowed to touch so much.

Frontline

It Is Like This

My days now start at 4am.

Pain wakes me.

I am an animal until I have medicated and sat still for some time. Maybe 30 minutes is the passage of time it takes me to travel from – the one that can only lurch dangerously around, sometimes falling, banging walls, and swearing, making animal noises, vaguely aware the neighbours are getting woken up for sure – to somewhere else.

Shame floats through like a lace fog.

My dreams are grim, and I know that is the drugs.

I have absolutely no memory of any other kind of sleep.

Last week in my Irish group, one of my sisters had tears spring into her eyes when I said that. She had been talking about having a medical procedure, having been through the rigours of cancer and emerged healed. She spoke of the difference between medicated sleep and normal, refreshing sleep. I had a sense of water flowing; clean, cold alpine water. Surely, I must have slept like an alpine stream once. There is no body memory of any such thing, ever. I wonder if I have forgotten, or if it has never been my experience, and it takes me to an abstraction where I don't feel real.

Back to real.

I am preoccupied with death – and while I know that's hardly news – there is a raw, urgent, often desperate quality running through these days and nights.

My time running out feels faster, and I feel an acute longing, infused with a desperation to finish this book. It's so nearly done; it seems impossible I'll not push it out before I run out of breath.

And yet this haunts me.

I am so impotently enraged to find myself again in escalating physical pain.
My right hip.
What can I say?
Heading for the X-ray department on Monday.

It's dark outside my BedWorld window.
I hear the rain.
I like the feeling of the sound.

Riding M

I wake up in my blue room.

It is winter – dark and lashing rain outside. I have beaten the alarm by twenty minutes. I am delighted to have done so.

I roll into the warm body of my lover. He is sleeping on his back, stretched out, arms akimbo, breath soft. I carefully unwrap the duvet and trace his skin with my fingers.

His cock wakes up before he does. I mount up and sit astride, sliding- oh-so-sweetly-down-onto him.

I crouch low, like a jockey racing for the winner's flag, and ride my lovely, hard and fast into Monday morning.

I kiss his sleep-sour mouth and feel him smiling into mine.

Funeral

It is such an honour to stand here with you all and speak at Jan's leaving do. In one of the Circles of Life that I call home we practice appreciating one another. This is an appreciation of Jan, a little prayer of gratitude.

I met Jan, not so many years ago, four, I think, on a 5Rhythms dance floor. I remember in my body – the dipping and swirling and twirling. I remember the smiling in both directions. I remember thinking, *Oh, I know you*.

I am so glad to be old, and maybe just about wise enough, to trust a bit of recognition when it occurs. Jan and I recognised one another as sisters, and got on with diving into that.

I am finding it so hard to start saying *was*. I want to say Jan is. Jan is funny, hilarious in fact, brave as a lion, demanding, as in asking you to be true even when it's tough to be so. She is, or was, so generous, loving, passionate and deeply compassionate toward all manner of our human messiness. I love her, or do I say loved her now? These semantics of loss.

My journey with Jan was coloured and often informed, but never defined by her illness. She lived with cancer a lot longer than I knew her. She absolutely lived. She believed in and committed to being alive. She would say life is wherever we are. Life is right here, now.

On November 1st 2010, when Jan's physical system crashed from a massive infection, and everyone said she would die, she didn't. I stepped into an act of devotion I had no idea I was capable of. For seven months every day was a dedication to Jan. I remember those first days and nights when I wouldn't go home – holding her hand, saying *Whatever happens you don't have to do it on your own*. I remember whispering over and over like a rolling prayer, all our names, the names of those who love her. I remember committing to stay, to bear witness, to accompany my sister until I couldn't go any further with her. I didn't know what I was doing. I was making it up.

I saw terrible things that had to happen to Janny's poor ravaged body. I learned more than I ever wanted to, and yet am somehow grateful for, about helplessness, vulnerability, being human, having a body, intensive care processes, tender and not so tender nursing practice. I watched and breathed and rooted for Jan, not only not dying as predicted on several occasions, but I watched her having to learn to breathe and speak, feed herself and go to the loo, stand up and walk – utterly basic things that mostly we don't even think twice about.

There was a particularly painful chapter when Jan was coming back to us for sure. She had things she wanted us to know and do. We were, on the whole, pretty crap lip readers, especially me she said. I think it was because she saw so much of me, rather than being the worst. But maybe I was.

Daniel was the best at it – he sweetly reminded his mum that it was her mouth that had taught him to speak in the beginning. She was so touched by that story she told it a lot. I'm telling it again for you Janny.

After over four months in hospital, she was sent home, to die really, though she proceeded to confound the doctors once again by turning her face back towards the sun. I went to stay for a while and it was such a pleasure to help in the practicalities, the cooking and cleaning, the things she wasn't strong enough to do. I do so cherish the sweetness of those months, even though Jan's life was on the line as never before.

As she strengthened, she dared to hope that she could and would make it to the bone marrow transplant. We talked of life and death, of wishes and kisses and fears and tears, and what if, and what if not. We planned to see Mr. Leonard Cohen sing in New York, and she spoke about the longing in her heart to meet a beautiful man, who would be her man to dance onward with. We also talked about food and telly and shopping. We read books together and stroked the big fat Minxy cat.

I loved being sisters like this. In the evening we'd take it in turns to do our ablutions and I'd set up my bed on the blue sofa. We'd kiss each other's dear faces and settle in. We'd talk, chunter. Often Daniel would arrive home smelling of young man smells, and he'd rock and roll around with us a bit and snuggle his mama and kiss me goodnight too. Sometimes I'd go off to the kitchen and return with Baileys (for Jan) and Limoncello (for me) and sometimes we'd fall asleep in the middle of a sentence and she would shout – *Take your glasses off Carolina*, or I'd tiptoe in to take her glasses off her face and tuck her in. Sometimes we'd crash around a bit in the night, dreaming, being scared, peeing. It was nice to have this company.

Jan could be impatient, and yet when the chips were down she had all the patience in the world. Early last year, I got myself into a mess of which I was so ashamed only one other person even knew. Jan showed up and loved me, and helped me and loved me so compassionately that in the end I believed her. What a gift. Priceless as they say on the Mastercard ads. My priceless Sister.

It wasn't nearly long enough to have found and lost a sister. For Jan to have lived so briefly and leave so soon, before she was done, well, as we know, it made her so mad. Yet in the end, as others have said, she gave us such a teaching on death and on life. She was tired of struggling in her ravaged body – of all the pain and more pain. She was ready to surrender and in those last few days had been able to say that to some of us. From many conversations over time that I have shared with her, I knew she was not so much afraid of death, but of dying alone.

She didn't die, or live alone. Our dear cherished Jan was cradled in the flow and presence of the love, intimacy and community, that utterly reflected her beautiful heart and the person she is, or damn it, was.

On the Friday when it became clear that time was short, people started flowing like a human river of love, to be with her, to say goodbye, to say thank you. Many deep breaths, a landscape of tenderness. For a while she was fairly clear what was what, who was there, who was coming. There was an exquisite moment when I found myself and Chloe sitting either side of her, and Chloe said *Shall we sing something*, and I said *Oh no not me, I'm such a frog!* And then the three of us, half whispering, half singing *Bravo Bravissimo*, a song we all know deep in our hearts from our dance family. Her sweet, trembly mouth singing this dear song. Thank you, God, for this. Thank you for all the tenderness of life, love and death.

She was a bit slurry and occasionally she slipped around in the here or somewhere else. Her pain was getting worse as was her breathing and they asked us if it was time to put her on the pump. Now I know what that question really means in palliative care terms. Someone said – *Ask Jan*, and she said, *Yes*. I hope she understood.

This how I remember it – a few of us sitting around her, and almost immediately after they had attached the pump, the last thing she said, and it was so very, very clear, was – *I feel I'm falling*. Cath said – *It's okay darling, you can fall, and we're all here*. Over some hours we sang and spoke about her, memories, gratitudes, prayers of all persuasion. Some Prosecco was drunk, some glasses raised.

Around midnight most people left for the night – three women and Daniel stayed for, as Linda called it, the Vigil. To stay until it was no longer possible to stay. As Jan dropped into the final waves of breath, where after such laboured breathing it became soft, almost imperceptible, like whispered breath. Daniel climbed onto the bed and wrapped his mama in his physical loving body, and we all held Jan and each other. Daniel said, soft as a son can be with his dying mother in his arms – *When you're ready Mama*, and she was.

In the utter mystery, and like the roll of a tide going out, she ran out of breath.

As soon as she died, she was smiling. A most beatific smile she left us with. It is, according to the experts, rare to die into a smile, but to me it seems very Jan, to fall into the mystery with her heart open and her mouth smiling.

It has been so extraordinary and so ordinary too, to travel with you, my longed-for sister. Someone said to me about a year ago, that I was brave to get so close to you when the likelihood of losing you was so high. Well, I don't know much for sure, but I do know we have to say goodbye to everyone, all people, places and things, so I try and practice saying hello with willingness to let my heart be broken over and over again.

Thank you for dancing and dancing with me Jan, and I always will be dancing with you.

As our Mr. Cohen wrote:
So come my friends, be not afraid – We are so lightly here.
It is in love that we are made – And in love we disappear.

Gone

i don't believe the dead speak to those of us left behind.

i don't believe you are out there on a cloud or a rainbow, looking down with loving protection.

i can't talk to you anymore, and although I do sometimes, I know you are not listening.

you are not talking back.

when I do hear you I know it's in the echo chamber of memory and longing.

you are gone.

Ashes

I keep an orderly house. Not in the tight, breathless way that used to be true. Now it is a soft-edged sort of order, but order nonetheless.

Recently in my orderly house, I found a white cat's whisker. It made me weep, this enduring cat's whisker.

It was Mr. Myrtle Moo's whisker. Moo for short.

He died in my arms last summer. It was a season of goodbyes, and left a distinct taste of love and loss on my tongue. I lost a cat and a sister and a cat, all in a roll over several short months. I was there each time, each moment for each last breath, each fall into the mystery.

For a while, it felt like all I loved had turned to ash.

Literally. I had boxes of ashes in my bedroom, and kept them there on the shelf until I didn't need to anymore. This wet summer, I sprinkled beloved cat ash into the garden where they had been cats all their lives. I folded the whisker into my hand, and then I let it fall.

A little later, very early on a pink dawn day, a small group of humans that had loved Jan dearly gathered on the edge of Hampstead Heath. We walked together across the ground that Jan had loved and walked, and talked, where her footsteps will always be, a small, disparate, threaded together little group, wandering and winding, coming back to the bag of ash that was once the human called Jan. Hands scooped out ashes and they fell and flew and slipped, each of us having our own intimate experience, separated, in the good company of simple love.

No one had much to say.

Too Much

I said goodbye to two cats and a sister.

It was a lot all in a roll.

I guess I did go a little mad.

I unravelled, prone to sudden storms of weeping no matter where I was.

Once I put my head down on a full trolly of shopping at a Sainsbury's checkout and started wailing.

They wouldn't let me pay with my Nectar points, and it broke me. I was ushered hastily out of the store with free shopping by several out-of-their depth managers.

It was like that.

It was too lonely day by day, seeing cats in the shadows and talking to photographs.

I went to the local animal shelter in search of mutual rescue.

The adoption officer had to fill in the five-page form while I wept and heaved out my answers beside her.

When she took me out the back to see the homeless, I asked her please not to show me any of the hard-to-place cats, the ones with complex multiple needs.

Just a little cat looking for a person, I said.

Forgiveness

Walking through early Sunday morning in my part of London. Not many people. Not much sign of the recent spring light that has been breaking through. A low, grey sky. Feet and paws going forwards.

Does the fact I have to keep forgiving myself mean I'm doing something wrong? Or that I think I am? I wrestle with this, and it's not so cut and dry. Not so simple.

There must be a part of me that yearns for a different life, another version of me. There must be, because I keep needing to forgive myself for being here like this. Maybe because depression is in itself such an unforgiving beast, I have to keep forgiving it?

An hour or so ago, with Leonard The Dog – lurching, stumbling, slouching, not toward Bethlehem, but just through the simple mechanics of another day. Park. Home. Leonard snoozing. Me – tapping out a postcard. Chewing on the word, the flavour of forgiveness. Dreaming of death, the way that I do.

I can do it.

First walk. Done.
An impulse followed through – a postcard or a prayer.
A batch of chocolate & peanut butter muffins (new recipe).

Second walk.
Bath (not negotiable as getting smelly).
PJs.
Food.
Netflix.

Made it through the day.

Sometimes I can't help judging my little life, for, well, being so little. I imagine myself much more productive and functional. I imagine myself with some of the stuff I will never have. Maybe, that's why forgiveness has to be an ongoing project? Maybe, we just have to keep forgiving ourselves, and each other, for being who we are?

Would I really trade myself up for one that didn't wake up every morning full of dread? Or one that wrote productively and socialised with ease? Oddly, I'm not at all sure I would. This is the one I am. I'd miss her.

The sort of forgiveness I'm tugging at is different from the radical forgiveness required in the face of violent acts, though radical enough in its own way. Forgiveness as a homecoming, as acceptance and love. Forgiveness as a celebration of being just like this. Forgiveness as a doorway to our own precious hearts.

I seem to have riffed my way into a kinder place. And the kindness, as one of my teachers once said, can hold everything.

As Leonard sings – *The sweetness restored* … not forgetting to include: *I'm tired and I'm angry all the time.*

It is all true. It all resides in the Fields of Mercy, Kindness, and Forgiveness too.

I'm here with my dog, pushing and pulling breath in and out of my lungs. It's my Sunday. It's my here and now. It is quite, quite simple, if I can let it be so.

I read Leonard The Dog my favourite poem penned by Leonard The Man and kiss the sweetest dog I've ever known. I sign off the windowledge and walk towards the muffins.

Small List

thimble
grain of sand
stamps
passport photos
cat's whisker
a rose petal
a fingernail

5am

I wake up weeping and wanking.
I so rarely feel that old heat and push and pulse.
It was like the weight and lightness of grief and relief – I thought surely, I'll sleep again now – but I'm awake and tapping.
Now and then with no warning, a big sob crashes up through my body and hits the walls of this benevolent room.

It's a thing, being a baseline depressive, having learned so much about how to roll with the drag and weight of it, and then to be hit by a depression tsunami. Oh man, I hear myself say – *Is depression really my home address? Because this is something else – this is being beaten up by depression.*

There are 20 raging men kicking, spitting, punching, shouting into my face the vilest of words. They get their cocks out and piss on me, shit on me, rub it in. They fuck me and beat me, and it never stops and somehow, I know I won't ever die, that I will just endure this violence, that it will go on and on and on.

This is what this depression feels like.

I dream of resting back into my bed of moss, the smells of summer and a bottle of pentobarbital.

What anchors me to basic functioning, to work, to moments of connection, humanity, to more than this?

What the fuck anchors me to anything?
I do still feel it.
Not feel it, but know it.

I'd like to feel it. I'd like to feel everything, and I am, as Leonard once wrote, greedy for nothing to feel. This is not nothing. This is something like agony, and if that's the word, that's a feeling I'd give up if I knew how.

I should say that this violent storm of depression beyond depression had a catalyst in the human relational world. A rude awakening, day(s) of reckoning, a climax to the unravelling that has been coming undone from mid-summer and turned on me like a gang of hate-filled men as another year in this terrible and beautiful world rolls open.

I loved and trusted.
Simple.
Eight years.
I didn't see what was completely there to see, until I had to.

The seeing began in the summer, and now is just seen.
I see.
I get it.

I am so tired of being in this body, so full of pain, so defeated, so desperate to slip out of these bones, viscera and skin, back into gone, mystery, nothing.

I also know it is not quite done, my little life.

Under attack from this super depression, I find this simple knowledge quite horrifying. Horror and peace. Strange bedfellows. I am not sleeping enough that's for sure despite my shameless medication. Pain in body and soul wake me up and I sit in BedWorld in early morning dark outside, overwhelmed that there is a day to stumble through; that on the clock doesn't start for several more hours, but mine has forced itself open.

Today I have five precious peeps to sit with, to be the safe for.

Falling away.

My whole life, it seems, is finding the courage to keep letting things fall away. When I say things, I mean ways I have understood myself, stories, ideas, beliefs.

They come up and bite my arse, but I am no longer capable of buying the narrative storylines. Something irreversible is happening, has been for a while, and I'm guessing will continue to roll. What, I wonder, will be left if everything I thought I knew about who I am falls away? Right now, here, as I tap on my laptop in the too early, I feel at peace with it; even as the brutality of this depression continues to go at me, I feel at peace with it.

I have a vision of Jan, as she breathed her last breath, ravaged by cancer, yet luminously all she was. Everything fell away, and what was left was clear to see, feel, understand, trust. I remember Alba-Maria being born. Her first breath. The same border, only opposite directions as one left and the other arrived. Everything that matters is right there, on that border. Part of me knows that border is life, not only the doorway into and out of.

Part of me knows that.
That is my anchor.

You could call it trust.

Out

I went out to salute very old friend and beautiful human – Polly McAfee, & her collaborator Cabby Laffy, at their book launch of second edition – *Love, Sex & Relationships*.

A sweet pleasure for a woman who doesn't get 'out' much. When I left the launch – and really understood what a palaver getting an Uber to find me in the middle of Theatre Land/Shaftsbury Avenue/ Charing Cross was going to be, never mind the cost which had been a bit mind blowing on the outward bound, even though I am a fully surrendered Uber Slut – I decided to take a deep breath and find my way to Charing Cross tube, on the Bakerloo line, all the way to my station.

It might not sound like much, but I haven't been on the underground, and barely a bus for must be seven years. Firstly, I got so physically broken I stopped being able to manage, initially just feeling too vulnerable out there in the seas of mass disembodiment, and then becoming literally unable to walk. Then COVID. My sense of direction is zero, even when I know where I am. But of course, my phone knows the way – she talked me through the streets heaving with human bodies, while I held the hand of my super adrenaline, verging-on-panic nervous system. As for going down those escalators, and along endless dirty white tunnels, following the signs to a platform. Jeeze.

I sit on the train, stunned by how the utterly familiar was feeling so loud and overwhelming – proximity to strangers, their smells, inadvertent physical contact, all the noise, the advertising shouting. Heart pounding, station by station, I arrive at Queen's Park. Daylight.

Remembering how there was a point when I just couldn't get up the stairs from platform to street, and now I can, though I still need to pull on the handrail and it is a slow, mindful climb.

A few minutes walking to my front door.

Home.
Unexpected epic experience.
Get breath back.
Take clothes off, soft, soft PJs, lots of dog kisses, cat head-dances, little fish supper. Fall asleep listening to audio book – will have to go back five chapters.

Home

Yesterday evening, returning to my little and cherished home to find Becci there, having been hanging loose with herself.

A blessing to be received into my own home, as it was to live with people for a few days. Awake just before 5am, not bad in relation to recent waking up literally in the middle of the night. Pain. What can I say? After a while, there is little more to say about constant pain. It is just here in constant companionship. Other people forget. For me just at this point, they forget less because it is more visible as I struggle up and down stairs, and wobble, lurch and stumble, unable to completely contain the sounds of my embodied experience.

Being on retreat – and at Anne's for the night and day before – I noticed the freedom I don't think about that much, to really give sound to the physical and mental pain I live with, especially, but not exclusively in the waking process, which as mentioned, is getting earlier and earlier. What a gift of freedom to let all those sounds be heard as they move through me – sobs, curses, groaning, shouting, it is all a part of what is mine. In company, I feel what it costs me to hold all that noise out of courtesy. Gratitude to my solitude for the freedom it brings. And gratitude for the occasional forays into sharing the business of being with another or others, in the physical presence of people to say goodnight to, wake up smelling coffee, and making my adjustment to volume control.

Returning in more ways than one from a death retreat.

A death retreat with Joanna.

Six years ago, I celebrated turning 60 years old by attending a death retreat with Joanna.

I feel the vast yet simple distance between these two retreats. I am so much quieter, know so much less, and am able to trust the freedom of not knowing so much more. Joanna is also six years further down the winding path of her precious life. There is nothing complicated in this, just deep, simple noticing.

I remember all the deep work with death I did with Massimo.

I remember Massimo – feeling his love and presence right now as I tap here in BedWorld – noticing light beginning to arrive outside my windows. Massimo; who once stood before me in the Tuscan woods at La Fontaccia, and told me he saw me as a father. He said – *You have great longing for your life, you are hungry. I see you.*

It was only then that I knew how much I'd needed a father who saw me. I needed that good father. My own father, in response to my running away from my legal and official home address aged 14, and was heard to say – *I don't suppose we'll see her again.*

I needed the father that would have come out to find me.

All those years later, I was redeemed in the loving gaze and understanding of Massimo's heart.

Men

I'm riding a Bakerloo train to meet a friend in the West End. Sitting in the rumble and screeching through the labyrinth under London, I'm not so much in train-world, but have gone somewhere else, drifting in the webbing and threads of what might become a poem.

A jolt at Baker Street, and I am back in the train. I notice my carriage is full now, and that all the seats around me are occupied by men.

I look. Really look – see and feel a whole landscape of men quietly being themselves.

There are three together, with toolboxes, paint splattered jeans, big boots. They fill up space, more than they actually occupy. Strong male energy, but also boy child, like a primary school playground. Their accoutrements are Lucozade, Coke and tabloids, yet also exuding the innocence of dirty knees.

In the adjacent seat is a very different man. He is polished and expensive; he smells of soap and something woody that makes me want to move closer and breathe in deeply. I feel my mouth smiling and catch sight of myself distorted and odd in the dirty, dark window across the centre aisle.

Next to me, requiring feeling rather than unabashed examination is a turbaned Sikh. He's reading a book and I want to know what it is. I imagine the question falling gently from my mouth. *What are you reading?* I say silently. I look at his legs stretched out in soft combat pants, his feet in white trainers. He is easy to sit beside which is not always the case. I like him, with no idea why.

I look some more and breathe in another brother. He's a little bit funk, with some hip, and a sprinkle of old hippie. He's listening to his iPod and I can see the music moving through him, though it's mostly internal and his body is still. I know he's dancing. His eyes are closed, his face is soft, yielding. I am moved to be seeing so much of him, and wonder about his life. In a soft-focus dimension, I imagine him having sex with the woman or man he loves.

Here is an old man. Very old. He is the mirror of everything that so many of us turn away from. I see beauty. He has a tremor, paper-thin skin, milky eyes, and like they used to say, no meat on his bones. I wonder about his life, so clearly drawing to its conclusion. I wonder if anyone else is seeing him. Looking around, I suspect not.

Here is a luminous angel and mostly no one has noticed. I take out my tiny moleskin, the smallest they make, and write the date, and then: I saw an Angel on the tube today.

Arriving at Piccadilly Circus – in awareness that it is still only men and me – even though some have got off along the way, and new ones got on. I drink in the anxious boy, the Rasta man, the American tourist, and the lost soul with his dead heroin eyes.

I see them all, and behind them I see ghosts and shadows – a moving collage of the lineage of men. I try and grasp something ephemeral as it slips through my fingers. That I've never really seen men, not fully. Another separation, an un-examined loss.

I give thanks to the weirdness of being called to offer myself to men in my blue room, to the courageous heart that beats in my chest, that said *Yes* to stroking naked men, nice and clear and simple, midst the cacophony of my noisy mind.

As I look around, I am singing inside, the place where I have a voice to sing with. *I know you now, I know you now, yes, yes, I know you now.*

Gratitude raises me up.
For the doorway swinging open.
For the gift of finding kinship with men – for the men that find their way into my blue hued world, and allow me to find and touch the naked underneath.

I give them my all.
They give me an opportunity to express and occupy my full wingspan of libidinal joy.
I get my day in the sun.

They get seen, welcomed, lovingly pleasured. Always touched, never handled. A little piece of each naked man resides in my heartland. I know there is a speck of my soul in each of them.

Baby Powder

I close my last Zoom room.
Throw off my clothes.
Heating on, windows open – forgive me planet, I won't get on a plane, but I can't do the cold inside thing.

Spray deodorant, sprinkle baby powder all over me and the bathroom, not because I smell, but because I love, love baby powder. My deodorant is baby powder, even the very expensive perfume I'm addicted to has a base note of baby powder – even poor Leonard The Dog has baby powder shampoo – I am delighted by the simple sensual joy of baby powder.

I start this day before my first client arrives – kneeling on the floor in my bedroom, as ready to go as a woman who woke at 3am can be, one who got furious for a while with being awake and then surrendered. I am shredding. I recently acquired a shredder. I'm slowly clearing the debris, gently, no rush, a little bit at a time, old tax returns, bank statements, client notes, case studies, all sorts of paper that I shouldn't just throw in the bin. It is nearly a clear deck. I think part of me is prepping for death. I'd love to leave a clean, clear space.

As I shred, I listen to political analysts discuss the possibility of world war breaking out. It feels like it just might do that. So much is breaking. I am not as politically literate as I would like to be, but I'm not uninformed. The global situation is almost entirely in the hands of power that is stronger and stronger in its resistance to ever letting, helping, encouraging, educating us humans to see and hear one another across difference and difficulty. We are being manipulated into splitting, not daring to think, to question, to strive to see the human in the so-called enemy.

There has been a little thread through some of my sessions today where the question of how to stay human, to not be devoured by the brutalities that belong to all of us if we can bear to know that. How to be helpless in boots and heart, how to stay and go and stay and go, but not have a triumph of total disassociation as the tool for survival. *How*, as someone I love once said, *to bow down to what is true, and breathe into everything anyway, as if your life depended on it, because it does.*

I'm here now, at what I consider the end of my day, though I appreciate some start getting ready to go out now.

I'm here in my PJs and baby powder cloud, canoodling with Leonard The Dog.

Anniversary

I remember arguing with Jan about 9/11. It was one of those rows about something else really. Suddenly triggered and fierce. I remember her face, how tired her skin was, and the shapes and movements of her mouth shouting.

I don't recall exactly what she said, something about the narcissism of America and how 9/11 has been bent and twisted politically to suit. I didn't disagree as such. I remember saying that, shouting that. I just mean the humanity of it touches me.

When the towers went down, I was deep in the Tuscan hills building a medicine wheel with a circle of old and new fellow pilgrims. We had been turned away from the modern world for several days and didn't know what was happening in New York or how the whole world seemed to be watching it on the television. I'll always be glad for that, to have been engaged in ancient ritual in good company at that particular moment in time.

Jan and I shouted up a storm about politics, life and death. It was a late afternoon in Tufnell Park. The light was fading.

Cancer slowly stealing Jan away from herself and away from me.

What do you mean? she yelled.

I mean, it haunts me, imagining the direct experience of being trapped up there in the burning sky. I imagine what it was like, what it must have been like, what it could have been like to choose to jump. All those people jumping and falling. To step out into space, to let go, to make that decision.

I stopped shouting.

I think about it. I feel it, the loneliness, the freefall, oh lord, I mean the mystery – what the fuck.

Suddenly we are both crying and laughing, and without warning we are both in forgiving tears.

I remember this as another 9/11 anniversary turns and she is still gone. I am grateful for that row. It is so vivid, and I feel how much I miss her in it.

Fall

Last Thursday, August 4th – I say the date because time has been shaken up into a new and more watery condition. I like water. The place I am most held – anyway, on that day, I fell very hard on my head, quite simply miss stepping in my garden off a very low wall. I thought I would find ground, but instead I found space and I fell, like a sandbag, hitting my head on a cast iron bench.

Concussion.

Strange, new country.

After managing to find someone to cancel my clients, I called 111. Not nice. Has no one thought about how to deliver this service to people, all in one way or another in distress? Rhetorical question, obviously.

Eventually, a person, questions = ambulance.
It felt excessive.
I felt embarrassed.

I had thought, with dread in my bones, I'd be told to go to A&E, but I sounded like I had/could have a brain injury, so A&E came to me.

Two incredibly relational, kind men arrive in my bedroom, and I am really seen, heard, and got.

I wept with gratitude.

They said I should really go to hospital with them for six to ten hours of monitoring.

I said, *I'd like to self/friend monitor here.*

They said – *Absolutely. It's lovely here – can we stay here?*

We agreed that I was stable, and my condition hadn't escalated, that I understood the red flags that could happen, and would call 999 asap if I started unravelling, that my friend would call every 45 minutes to make sure I still knew what day it was.

Did I say how kind they were?

I felt fathered and brothered. One young Aussie, and one older dad/bloke kind of chap.

I didn't work for a week.

I'm working gently this week – a precious person is landing in my Zoom room soon.

This is a little impulse to check in, to say, *Oh here I am, I've been somewhere, and I'm still coming back.*

Like any going any somewhere, we come back a little bit different. I'm tasting the different, like the space where a tooth came out. I lost something, though I couldn't tell you what – and it feels like a blessing, not something I need to get back.

Spring

dog repetition
he takes me out and back in
three times everyday

Heels & Healing

Once upon a time, a light-lifetime ago, there was a girl that could run in high heels. She ran the streets of Sydney at night. If I half close my eyes, I can see her there still.

Still running.

Once I ran around in high heels and tiny clothes.

I was tiny then. It may have been the intravenous drug and Mars bar diet that kept me small.

Maybe it was the drugs, or my relative youth, or maybe the angels or drag queens that kept me on my feet.

I ran around those nights in Kings Cross, Sydney, Australia, selling my pussy, my mouth, my arse, and never once falling off my stilettos.

The thing is, thirty years later, a woman that eventually learned to walk on the ground beneath her feet, has lost the art of dancing like a tiny drug-fucked gazelle, on impossibly high heels.

It wouldn't matter that I had – if I hadn't had a vision of myself wearing shoes to make your eyes pop out – on the occasion of my approaching fiftieth birthday.

My Mum

It really is the baby me, the one beyond words, only embodied memory and experience that is coming home now. She feels a lot, has carried a lot.

My mum was severely psychologically ill, yet functioned well enough on top. She ticked all the boxes for borderline/narcissistic personality disorder.

Being hated – an experience I breathed in from the very first breath, even from being conceived – she didn't want children. It revolted her, but lived in a class and historic context where there was no choice really, unless you were an outrider and she certainly wasn't that.

The sexual abuse happened when I was tiny, and wasn't weird perverted doing stuff to me. With the hindsight and understanding of such things, I can see she was unconsciously self-soothing. She rubbed herself against me, arousal but not to orgasm, the way you might with a pillow or your own hand. I imagine she was so unaware of me as a separate being that she didn't even realise that often I was squashed, breath and swallowing restricted. It didn't matter. I didn't matter. I wasn't real to her except as an object, mostly repellent, sometimes as a tool for comfort.

I believe/know that this stopped around the age of two, as I started to become more obviously separate, learning words. This early experience is deeply embedded in the baby bones and dust of me.

I've worked through so much along the road.

This is the very beginning of me, being received at last in the body. Blessed by all the circles of love, the cranio miracle, my people, my kin, you – having a place in the world. Knowing and trusting I am seen and loved.

I both grieve and salute my sexual history.

I acted out a lot of what I learned back there. For many years, I allowed anyone to do anything they wanted to me, much of it quite unspeakable.

I found my way to some kinder places, including being a part of the gay male S&M scene in Sydney. They kind of adopted me, and somehow it was less terrifying on the level of intimacy, though I didn't understand that then. It was just healing.

In partnerships, I have always found myself fighting for breath in sexual intimacy.

My exquisitely redemptive chapter of Stroking Naked Men, the libidinal homecoming.

Seven years of holding space and welcome for erotic pleasure through connection, deep naked heart, and undefended presence. Not entirely unlike the work of psychotherapy. Held by the form, I was right there. It was a wild calling and a great gift.

I gave a lot of erotic tenderness to many beautiful men, met an ocean of lonely and was allowed to touch it, and love it.

I was free, and was healed in this devotional service. I gave and received. My ravaged sexuality had her glory years.

Do I feel sad knowing I am not capable of the proximity of partnership?
Yes.

Do I feel peaceful about it?
Yes.

Fragile

The fourteenth of each month is the anniversary of Grenfell burning.

It's like a reflex in my nervous system, and I just wrote the date and felt the sucker punch.

It's not my topic, but I couldn't not thread it in.

I don't know what my topic is, except the fragile connection to my roots in this earth.
Here I am.
I am here.

These are strange days of falling. I am not unfamiliar with falling, but falling in recent years has felt more fluent, even included threads of graceful. The falling has often had coherence, whereas this falling is much more akin to losing it.

What are we really talking about when we say losing it?

What am I talking about?

What is there to lose?

I do feel myself as the thinnest, most delicate, cracked white porcelain. I am a vessel and every part is tiny cracks. The fact that this vessel holds its shape, is a miracle of sorts and a definite altered state.

I'm weaving this into my long labour book; this solitary experience of falling.

I have things to say, though to paraphrase Kae Tempest, *They have all been said and felt before*. We are all so ourselves, and also so connected in our universal human experience.

I believe we are all falling.

As I tap away, I feel the contact with my own mad, messy me-ness, start to return. I am indeed here.

Like this.
This primal lost.
It is not nothing to keep trusting, losing the trust, withstanding the awful sensation of being a breath away from shattering – yielding to another wave of trusting that I can actually feel.

I veer between peace and longing, and a kind of panic as my mind tatters.

Reality check – this is the madness of severe under-sleeping.

I am awake again. 24 hours has rolled around and I am here again in this special quality of very early morning solitude. It is the middle of the night really.

Holy and Hilarious Work

Six am in my cabin at the top of Fanny and Colin's wild and sloping garden.

This little book is a much slower walk than I imagined, but if history is a reference, then I am walking as I do when making writing.

Here in Devon.

Away from home for the first time since 2018.

A spike of judgement stabs my foot – my oh so little life.

It passes through.

Bowing Down to what is True: the name of Fanny's Retreat.
I have been lonely for kinship in the physical world.

I have ached for the radical simplicity, shared experience.
The leaning is like nothing else is.
It takes my weight.

I am in the community of undefended heart, nourished by the depth and simplicity of this holy and hilarious work.

Coming on retreat is like the neighbourhood gathers and offers each precious piece of what matters to the circle. It is healing and redemption in action. As I tip-tap away in the pre-light, hearing the wildlife outside my cabin instead of London waking up, I thank Life for all the Circles over all the years since I came to, crash landing into the community of Narcotics Anonymous.

I wouldn't have made it without all these circles of ragged stones.

It has been far too long.
I know I am walking towards the end of it all, my life a prayer, and my 'success' is having stumbled home despite so much blood on the walls.

My goodness, the well of my resources was dry.

Don't leave it so long. Go a lot. Go as much as possible. Give yourself a lot of village caro.

Got Home. Key turns, door
Opens. Re-entry happens
Welcome Home Caro

Help

gawd, dear Lord
I am in a weeping and wailing country
it is the deepest strangest experience of skinned alive – and free
i must write
Time is getting shorter
I must write
I write

What If

what if this is the dance?

what if I have to lose everything?
what if this is the dance?

these words, trying to be something, broke through binge watching The Morning Show. I pressed pause and took Leonard for a pee, as usual at this time, in my pyjamas.

what if this is the dance?

so much everything – my sorry sorrow, the world, the injustice, the hopeless, hapless business of being a person. Dead babies and puppy farms, all of us in the hands of the few – my little life – our little lives.

what if this the dance?

the hell and homecoming of so much falling away – especially so much of what I believed I held lightly, only to learn, continue to learn in a series of cars crashing into walls – that I was holding with an iron grip.

what if drinking Diet Coke to get through the day and taking a pill to sleep at night, is the dance?

what if I am here like this, beyond guilt or innocence, or the lineage of addictions and incest, because this is the dance?

what if every time I shed another layer of skin and think I understand something, it disappears? Am I lost again?

found?

nothing makes sense.
everything makes sense.

this is the dance.
this is the dance.

Wings

I write from despair and desperate, which somehow in the last hour moved from alone to enfolded. What a difference those wings make, the cradle of that enfoldment. So battered and so beautiful.

Just for location, orientation: I am in Devon, with a small group of fellow travellers, with Joanna at the helm. It took everything I've got and more to get here. I nearly gave up. I often give up, just because the effort feels too much. It might be *pass the salt*. It might be getting somewhere and getting back.

I am daunted by the projected getting back, which actually doesn't start for nine more hours. I am here, I am noticing the projecting myself part, and I am able to love her. I am touched by my own human descent out of this moment and my capacity to call her back to this moment, imperfectly, but good enough.

I dozed over the laptop, waking fully again just now.
I have grit and tears in my eyes.
I can hear other humans moving and smell coffee.

In a minute, I will drag myself into clothes and lurch to morning sitting. Tomorrow when I awake (whatever time it is) I will be in my own good company, with Leonard and Bebe. Neither of them drink coffee.

Sometimes – because it's a choice, the only way for me – I give myself up to the luxury of missing this, the waking with others.

Tears in my Eyes

Maybe this is it – my little life with tears in my eyes
and the ocean of tears in my heart?

In my idea, the way that line, inspired by the man I call Kevin,
In my idea of it, this living with tears in my eyes,
it looked like Kevin.

I should say I love Kevin
& when he weeps, it is like an act of nature happening,
a stream of luminous water falling down his face.

He dabs at his face if there's a tissue to hand,
or sometimes an actual hanky made of cloth is retrieved from a
pocket, as he lets this act of natural beauty happen till it's done.

He doesn't make a song and dance.
I think of the day he gifted me this title
which was some years back in our ragged circle of stones.
He'd said something like – there are tears in my eyes, and then they
flowed down his Kevin face until they were done for that moment
of being Kevin, with us.

I remember he didn't know why they were happening,
and going home at the end of that particular Friday, to write:
I aspire to live with tears in my eyes, on my list of titles.

I have many titles of poems, books, articles, mostly unwritten.
There is so much unwritten writing inside me,
writing that would have loved to be born
closer to truth; longed to be born.

Writing this now, my tears are falling, with no finesse
much more of a mess, to be honest.

And, I notice there is healing happening, but not 'noticing' so hard that healing happening becomes a thing, and then healing happening stops.

I'm just here, the morning after Groupies Friday,
always a new morning after, but always felt
as the morning after our Friday together, with Tim.

I count my precious paying humans and there are five.
I thought there were four.

A little overwhelm happening, and I say it out loud,
Overwhelm happening.
I have learned if I do that thing, say the word
followed by happening, something happens inside me.

I suspect, being a psycho and all, that I hear and feel myself,
just happening in this moment, and I feel my own cradle,
my battered wings enfolding the overwhelm, or whatever
other feeling might be there, just looking for a place to feel welcome,
a place to rest her head in that cradle: always there if she remembers
to remember.

A poem is happening,
A poem with little effort to craft it, more a willing
to trust it kind of poem.

There are poems and poems.
This one is heart jazz impro, a little thing finding its own way
onto an empty Word document page.

Living with tears in my eyes requires a rescue mission
without a map,
a brutal self-love
the courage (& faith) to see the brand new-born me –
no, not the baby, the actual first breath of me
the unremembered landing into sadistic absence.

a life-long trail of bloody, broken homing pigeon
until I could truly meet, recognise and, yes, rescue that one –
the one that didn't know she made something so longed for, true,
in places where it wasn't true.

I haven't fixed myself
I haven't arrived anywhere in particular
I just rescued that tiny fragment of rage, need and delusion.

I saw her trapped in the hopeless of making up stories
(& believing them)
of what she'd needed, like all us newbies do,
to be got, received, felt.

That homing pigeon part, to give her her due
had brought a lot of unremembered home.
She builds a house on kind ground, and it is real.

She just didn't see until she could, the shard of desperation to be got,
to be read like a book already written.

She had made it true in a few critical human attachments
the technical word for love and connection
& truth be told; it wasn't really there.
And when that indescribable storm tore the house from the ground
whatever kind that ground had been and held.

Yes, it was then, she allowed
her homed and homeless self,
to be shattered, broken, destroyed, blown into non-existence
and all the not true, longed for being got, by the other,
by the Mother,
finally fell away.

She got down on the dirty floor and picked up this desperado newborn
even though she was tired as hell, and partly
just didn't want to – it was time and it was right.

It was simple, unequivocal,
it knew how to pick up that tiny shard of desperation-to-be-got,
and to get her.

She took her home
to where the cradle
woven out of battered feathers, moss, some blood & broken, earth, sand,
a few stars borrowed from the darkest night sky,

was already there, waiting to receive her
and did receive her
she lives there now.

My somewhat delusional, beautiful, lyrical heart
would love to tell you
that these rooms are always full of light, that peaceful
and freedom are easy.
It's not like that
It is home.
It is a cradle for the newborn and the babies.
It is safe, especially when that doesn't feel true.
It is where all is welcome, seen and loved, without condition or contract.
Even and especially when that doesn't feel true.

It is where I have slipped inside the skin of Mother & Father both, the ones I needed nearly 66 years ago,

even and especially when that doesn't feel fair.

Fury

death opens the double doors wide –
I see a vista of nothing.
it is unbearable to keep walking,
stumbling with a fucking stick,
towards this big empty, holy invitation
to dive out of this bloody, beaten body

and fly, fall, disintegrate, become dust
I cannot make a sound, a poem,
or the ugliest of movement.
I cannot convey my direct in this moment experience.

If I could – I would be throwing myself against walls
and screaming: *I have had enough now.*
Please God take me somewhere called nowhere.
Fast, urgently, the opposite of life support.
Death, death – put her on the death machine.
Make it all stop.

Macaroni Woods

I sit in my not-at-home bed at Macaroni Woods, here for the us that is my Long-Group annual weekend. We go away together with Tim.

Two nights. This is the morning of the second. Later today we disband, and D oh so kindly drives me and all my paraphernalia home.

My paraphernalia these days, in order to go anywhere, is hefty. Huge beanbag plus assorted support cushions, pregnancy pillow and soft blankets.

Disappointment happening, given that it is June, that it is cold. I brought my delicious, new from the charity shop near my Cranio Sacral venue in Primrose Hill, boxy, linen tunic dress. Primrose Hill is wealthy London, hence the quality stock of their charity shop. My frock is quirky, suits me. Inside it with just underwear, with my feet in the Crocs that raise me up with the block sole, and encase my feet so I don't fear falling, I look good.

It's pink.

Pink that works.

Across the top are horizontal stripes, then the main body of this dress becomes a solid, soft pink. I wanted to wear it with my groupie family. Instead, I brought it into the big room where we 'group' and laid it out to be seen, imagined with me inside it.

This group is a place I call Home.

Not the core home. That home is inside me, finally fully occupied.

This place is one of the homes that has helped, beyond any words that could do it justice, my bloody pilgrimage to my own sweet self. I have been in this group since it began. It is what people in the psycho business call a 'slow opening group', meaning it is a continuing journey rolling onwards. People make a commitment to stay for one full season, after which, if and when someone leaving wants to happen; it is thoughtful, included, and a period of leaving is woven into real time.

We have been a solid long-staying constellation for some years, with no exits and new incomers. We have just said goodbye to K, and he is not here – there is another leaving happening. We will not be the same constellation next year at Macaroni Woods, so there is a particular quality of us, separately and as an us, feeling the direct experience of that together.

As for me.

I am finally able to give up any semblance of disguise. I am absolutely broken, and discovering the difference between showing up undefended but still partially hidden, and showing up utterly stripped to the bone. Part of my mind is whispering that I had no choice, but I know there is always a choice to be hidden where most broken is happening, or to allow full broken to be seen. It is

trust that makes allowing possible. It is ever so simple, but a bloody hardcore journey to build enough trust, to then allow.
I have been a devoted pilgrim.

All of me lives at my house now. All of me. At the end of the day, every single micro cell of all I am comes home with me. So, I trust me enough to trust you, without the condition that if I trust you, you will get me, attune to me. I can even long for that, and not get it, and from the luminous, bloody truth of being my own home address, still trust you love and want me.

Yesterday, in the group, as a pose to the spaces between, E was taking some space at the same time as I was desperate to bring something in. Do you know, I can't even remember what, just that it was so hard to hold it, to yield to E, to wait it out, to stay.

E says *You're distracting.*
I agree and try to be less distracting.
E says *It's like you are having a breakdown in the room.*

I am triggered in a heartbeat.
I hear –
Not okay.
Not welcome.
Mad.
Too much.

I am bellowing.
I am having a fucking breakdown in the room.
Been having a breakdown in the room for months, alone.
Holding my broken and lonely and feral alone.
I am here having a fucking breakdown in the room, still accountable as best I can; to it is all of us, not just me.

You get the gist.
I lost it.
Big trigger.
Big shouting.
In reality it was short.
Tim did what I would do in my group. He came and brought me in from the storm. He settled and anchored me here, through the doorway of contact and breath.
It is simple to tell E I know he didn't say anything except what was true, and that it took me, at sonic speed, to all the places of not okay, and not wanted, and reductive diagnostic homelessness.

I am not entirely sure he fully gets what a gift it was to be triggered into that storm of bellowed pain and rage.

Testosterone

I started micro-dosing testosterone as a possible ally in the medicinal protocol that helps me manage the constant physical – which or course informs the mental – pain I live with.

I gave it a fortnight. I did feel a little more mental focus, stamina and general mojo, including some libidinal desire. I've put it back in the cupboard though, as I've also been experiencing the constant throb of anger.

Angry and horny.

Not fun.

Grateful

Ha.

We are supposed to understand something, and then it all becomes clear that there is nothing to understand. Nothing to understand, but still here; washing clothes, paying bills, perplexing people who are horrified by the what-if-there's-nowhere-to-get-to-because-we-are-already-here position.

Thank you for your love, for picking up the weird and wonderful technology that makes such a shared moment possible, for being so you, while I am so I – it is grace.

Today I am grateful for various things:
You.
Sun.
Breeze.
Cancellations resulting in only one paying human, while the others pay me anyway.

The sounds of my shell wind chimes.
Pain medication.
Leonard & Bebe.

That even though it all went wrong, there is still only one word on my tongue – it is of course, Hallelujah.

Love from the softest place, deep in the centre of bruise happening.

I remember all those years ago, sitting beside my heart sister Jan, in the ICU at the Royal Free. Just her in her coma, me, and the most wonderful, and remarkably young Irish nurse.

She spoke to Jan as if she were awake and listening, and was confused and frightened. She had the sweetest (not sugar sweet) voice, and she saw Jan. She saw her, and she did her work from that place. She saw me too. There we were, three humans in the middle of a night in early 2011, being with what was.

A moment happened.

She looked straight into my heart, of this I have no micro speck of doubt, and she said – *Why don't you put your head down. It's okay. You keep her hand in yours, but just rest your head on the bed beside your sister.*

I put my head down.

I realised later I'd been waiting my whole life to hear those words. To hear those words, to receive them, to truly put my head down for the very first time.

I have forgotten her name.

I saw the best and the worst that we humans can be during those long weeks beside Jan, never really understanding where she was, or if she would come back (she did for a while).

It is where I was able to receive the longed for, without even knowing it was a longing, invitation to put my lonely head down.

Sometimes I offer that invitation to another, sometimes that other can receive it. Sometimes not.

Because of that moment, I can, and do when my heart remembers just how simple it can be, offer it to myself.

Today I can hear/feel and lean into the enfoldment of my generous wingspan, and rest my head.

I love you.
I feel loved.
How radically simple is that.

Dear Reader

I am beginning to check out, though it will be a little longer than the 'check out' two minutes or so we are invited to occupy at the end of a group, a retreat, many a gathering of humans that concludes in a circle, inviting each voice to speak so we hear ourselves at the end, as an us or a we, more than the sum of its parts.

There are many voices in this collection of postcards and riffs, mostly the voices of different parts of messy old me, with some that took up residence in my internal world for periods of time, before I understood they were not mine at all. Those ones have over the years been recognised and shown out the front door. Off you go, I say, back to live in your own house.

When I began to assemble this little book, in my imagination it didn't take much time at all. Of course, as with everything, it is so utterly different, the imagining and the real experience. Plus, I am a lumbering slow. It is my natural pace.

There is a little corner in my mind where I have an idea of myself as light as a feather, where I dance so lightly through this little life of mine. I leap across fences, across spaces and distance, onto the bare backs of magical horses. I love the felt sense of this me, the one that only exists in dreamed me. In real me, I am heavy footed, and heavy of heart. I lumber, stumble, fall and crawl. Perhaps every human has these other ones inside?

I also have one that can sing.
I mean really sing.
She does not exist in this world.

I began in 2021 just as lockdown was opening up, thinking I would spend a few months assembling the fairly meagre (quantity wise) collection of what Leonard C. always called his scribbled life. He had a massive scribbled life, and still said it pained him that he hadn't devoted more of himself to writing. My scribbled life will always break my heart for being so unwritten.

I do wonder if after death you cut me open and examined the physical inside, there might be multitudes of words unwritten scratched into bones, stacked up in muscle, and swimming through blood into organs, gathering in the ravaged chamber of my heart so full of longing for all the unborn writing.

Tears are happening as I tap, suggesting sad is happening, suggesting I just hit a bit of true.

My goodness, there is so much simplicity to lay back into.

I wish I had known that sooner.
I wish it had been my original home ground, that I hadn't needed to spend a whole lifetime arriving into simple and welcome.

It is regret.
Grief actually.

I think of my mother and remember most of all her martyrdom, the way she positioned herself on the cross of suffering. It is a passive–aggression position. I've been there. I mean I lived in that position, my version, for a lot of my life. It feels like a waste, but is just loss and cost, and that I made it out the other side. The truth that I won't be exiting on that cross is my ever so humble success story. I know that's true because the tears are rolling, with no speck of blame or sour and bitter.

Just grief and gratitude.

I went to Devon, to the village. Restoration.

It is just hard to come home, to miss the refuge, and to know I am my own refuge. It is also hard to feel the space I have created. This longed for, hard won spacious, that will be where I live until I stop living. I find myself face to face, heart to heart, with this one. I am here with this one. Of course. And she/I will never be a different one, a better or worse one, just closer to and kinder to this broken open pilgrim that carries heavy in her DNA.

What's next?

& again

Another ridiculous early, middle of the night new day beginning.

Facebook threw a scrap of 2017 at me. I remember the feeling of writing this. I touch myself.

a little bird
took wing –
for a moment
the confines
of my well traced
bedroom ceiling
broke open
I was flying
like I'd been
flying all my life

Work

I'm back at work.
Back in the therapist's chair (though it's never a chair).

My new shape of work and not work. New spacious. New balance. New taste. Entirely new taste.

Here I am, tasting – in between being with one human and the arrival of the next.

Muse

I love that word, muse/musing. I always have, but in a recent essay for *Advantages Of Age*, I began with the sentence – I've been musing on losing, and I felt it as sensuality.

I stop.
This moment.
Musing on sensuality. Mine. My sensuality.
I sit here in my semi-mangled, nearly sixty-six-year-old body, the one that is pulsating with pain, and ponder the deep sensuality of my nature.

Oh yes, a space opens up as I tap into this vein of musing. I am an unfathomable sensualist. I'd almost forgotten the wonderful of this part of me. Not exactly forgotten, as it just is. I have been drifting away from direct contact with the wide and the deep joy of it though, and am having a quiet and unexpected reunion with myself right now.

The room is full of light.

I have shell chimes in the softest medley of blues hanging in my open window. They sing in the breeze.

I am wearing my favourite pyjamas. When I say pyjamas, I don't refer to the classic kind. Much of my 'bed-wear' is not actually bedclothes. I have a large collection of clothes that are pyjamas in as much as I change into them at the day's end. If you rustled through my pyjama basket you would know I'm a sensualist.

These are actually pyjamas.

A camisole vest and crop length wide drawstring bottoms. They are also blue hues, and the softest of soft cotton fabric. I have dressed myself in the quality of tenderness. There is I realise, quite a lot of tenderness in my wardrobe.

Towards an Ending

I have been a month with no words for this ending, the wrapping up of my postcards from a little life. I am not quite signed off.

Words have failed me on the page.

There is such agony in not writing and there has been so much not writing.

Right now, in this very moment, this moment that as I name it slips out of this and into that moment. I mean, that's enough to blow a tiny mind. We are literally experiencing time slipping away with each and every breath.

This moving moment then, I show up again on my empty page and realise it is almost one month of moments since I was here.

In this moving moment, I am emerging from the journey through last night. It was exceptionally stark. I am seeing as if through a lens of forensic awareness, turning off my television at approximately 11.15pm.

I had taken my night medication an hour earlier. I take a slow-release pain pill, a sleeping pill, and my new antidepressant.

I was lying very still on my back with both my hand and the remote control on my chest. I wish I was more often able to desist from this habit with my television at night.

I wish a lot of things.

It is however, a kind of art to catch the moment I am losing consciousness and use agency to press that button that blanks the screen tucked back into the shelf at my bed end. If I don't, it will shut down. I don't wake up with it still running, a parallel universe that I am not in sync with. No, I don't like that at all.

It is different though, to catch myself falling into medicated sleep, in time to do the switch-off. I caught it last night. It means that I then rearrange my body into a more sleep supporting shape, taking a pillow away, curving a little off flat into semi side, with a pillow supporting my front and Leonard pressed light against my back.

Last night I got it.

I sleep for about two hours, waking in acute pain and the pressure of needing to piss.

It requires I get up, travel down my hall to the bathroom. It all hurts. Sometimes I weep. Sometimes, even though my bladder's full, I can't find the on tap. Sometimes I doze off while waiting, which is horrible.

Last night, I pee.
I stumble back to bed.

My small hallway, at night becomes something to be endured.

I do drop back down into something like sleeping, though semi-aware. I feel the building up of pain and pressure until it is necessary to clamber up again. To repeat. I am weeping and whimpering. I make it back. I try and rearrange my body into bearable. I can't find bearable so I bear it.

It is approximately 2am.
It is too much.
I get up and take half a sleeping pill.
I have half a pee.
I try again.

Sleeping takes me somewhere.
I dream something I cannot remember, but I can feel.
My nervous system shakes.

I wake again.
It is approximately 3.45am.
Body is screaming.
I weep by the open fridge door.
I take another pain pill.
Back in bed, I pray for mercy.
I drop.
Waking up, as in this is it – a new day – gifts me with an almost unheard of 7am.

I wake up sobbing.
I am here, more or less.
I feed the non-humans.
Take beginning of day pills, stumble back to BedWorld.
Kiss Leonard.
Sniff Leonard.

Shed tears on Leonard.
Thank Leonard for being with me.
Tell him he snored a lot.
Tell him I love him.

Somehow, I have found my way back to this unwieldy checking out.

I would like it to be as linear as saying it has been hard these past few weeks, which is true but not linear. In some respect it is always hard. It is my relationship to hard that weaves, struggles, yields, picks up the fight again, tires me out to the point of despair, takes me away from everything, until that is so painful I have to give up and bring defeat back to the welcome mat.

Desperation happening.
I prefer sad happening.

Writing is part of bringing me back to connection – back to the place where I feel. I am here now. Feeling.

Such a dance I do with feeling and not feeling.

I might have mentioned before that I listen to music less than you might think. As with writing, the music I go to is all about contact. I don't, actually can't, have music without feeling it. No background for me. It is always foreground.

When I emerged from my murderous addiction, I could not listen to any music at all for about four years.

Even now after many more years, to put on music is a choice to meet and open to the one I am with.

I am heavy as hell.
I am tired as all hell.
I am lurching between the pain of not feeling, the longing and resistance to feeling, and getting through these days and nights of life slipping through my fingers.

I also feel new freedom in this very old storyline.

There is space, literal, concrete space, which in my magical thinking part, I imagined like a longed-for holiday – that then turns out to be you as you are in a different location.

I have to say it's something like that.

I am grateful, and even a little bit proud of having managed to create new space that will hold, and I find myself in it feeling the disappointment (and the comedy) of disembarking from the plane in a new place, finding I am still here with all that is. It still hurts like hell.

The freedom is more internal new space, where I seem to have lost the capacity for making myself a problem to solve. That is a huge joke. A joke I'm full of gratitude to be able to appreciate.

In coexistence, in this freedom, is everything.
If freedom means I can't get a head of steam going to make a drama or a problem, the everything just is, moving and grooving in the spacious of free.

Hilarious and often, at least for now, unbearable.
I am getting acquainted, anew, with the continents of unbearable.

To quote Leonard the man, not dog: *The crisis was light as a feather*. Funny how heavy that light as a feather can be.

Done

Dear Reader,

I am done.
This postcard jigsaw.
This weave of fabric.
This labour of love, struggle, surrender and trust, is done.

Maybe ten days ago I got it.
I mean, I heard it.
I noticed I was in struggle with the words on the page, and deep in the river of simple, flowing as ever underneath any and all noise, I heard the whisper of true.

Let struggle fall away.
It is this.
It is done.

It did not feel triumphant.
It didn't feel much of anything at all.

Given I was tuned into river frequency, I could hear – step away.

I stepped away.

I let Rose know I was done except for reviewing the totality of what I'd made before handing over, as I always do with my writing to Rose.

It is the biggest thing I've ever handed her.
I proposed that I do handing on the fifth of October – my sixty-sixth birthday. I do like a bit of symbolic.

I was feeling sluggish. Depressed. Disappointed not to be swinging off any chandeliers.

I stepped towards and started reviewing these pages.
Sluggish woke up.

Having spent the last three years making this book into a book – having thought it would take a few months to bring it together. Having been heard to say often. Too often. I got on my own nerves – repetition: it's nearly done.

Now it is done, and I am inside what I have made, checking it out for pre-Rose tweaking. I am inside what I actually made – I am now awake, not sluggish.

I have made a something, bringing threads and fragments of old into non-linear shape and form. Through this runs the river of my here and now voice. This voice.

I am reading myself, tweaking as I go, rearranging a few pieces of the collage, taking some bits out altogether. I read me again.

October 2024
London, UK

Acknowledgements – Gratitude

Without Rose Rouse this little book would never have been born – not only in the beautiful job she has done in editing it, but the friendship, belief and encouragement she has offered to my tiny scribbled life over nearly two decades, that has always made it better and given my words some muscle definition. Thank you doesn't feel enough but it is all I've got.

Asanga Anand for my beautiful watercolour art – these small pictures make my heart sing. You got inside each moment they represent, listening to what I said, much more than referencing the photographs I provided you with.

Fanny Behrens and Colin Harrison. Colin is certainly not going to be in the world when this book sees the light of day. As I write these words, he is doing justice to his life, to all he gave and all he touched, by dying with his beautiful heart wide open. Thank you, Fanny and Colin, for the generous and radically simple work of Movement of Being – for all the ways you have left your marks on me.

To Natalie Miles, because you help me way beyond the remit of the work that I pay you for. You have become a friend over these long years as you come every week to help me keep my house in order.

To Dani, Rodrigo and Pedro. Thank you for being Familia, for being a second home for Leonard, for your kindness, generosity and love. I cannot imagine life without you all.

To Paul, Maureen and Genna. Well, for being my family, for seeing me as I am, and for loving me as I am.

To Emma PB, for being a luminous thread of connection – heart to heart – soul to soul.

To Marci – love and gratitude – always.

To Amanda Player, for holding me in the deeply intimate supervision that helps me hold the precious humans that entrust me with their vulnerability, and allow me to see and touch what matters.

To Andrew Hassenruck, for both the friendship that delights and sustains me – you are a part of my village – also for the work we have done together. The beauty of your filming, in which you are pure presence and invitation. Thank you for filming me.

Becci – you are one of the few, where together we can both say – "I know" and it means everything.

To Shaun, for being a buddy and friend to Leonard The Dog every weekend so he gets the miles he needs.

To VP for helping me bring the very last, and most desperate shard of homeless in from the cold.

Fee – for being such a significant part of my landing back in the UK and finding my feet – and for taking me to the desert where you have built your home and your life. Thank you for the poetry that infuses all the buildings you make; for being so you, the way that you do.

Jess Glenny, thank you for the wonderful words you offered to the beginning of my book – and for all the resonance. All that dances between us, so distilled. So precious.

To Doctor Amanda Craig, for being my GP for over three decades, and for seeing, hearing, and caring for me the way that you have and do. You are one of my reparative mums.

A bow to all the poets and singer-songwriters that have been, and still do, help me feel and remember what matters. Kae Tempest and Leonard Cohen, since I have referenced them both in these pages, and to Sean Taylor because he keeps getting me out of the house to come and hear him do his beautiful, undefended thing in small, old-school London music venues.

Anne Aubin – you know why.

To Clare and Alba-Maria McClure. For everything. For always.

To York Publishing Services for being absolutely who I needed to help me publish this book on my terms, with all the understated expertise, professional approach, and for being a beacon of light in the sea of utterly bewildering chaos the self-publishing market place is.

To all the fellow pilgrims that have been, either for a fleeting moment, or in it for the long dance, for being with me in the mystery of THIS.